Gifts from GRIEF

Gifts from GRIEF

A journey back home

Rachel Pope

Gifts from Grief
Rachel Pope

All rights reserved
First Edition, 2019
Copyright © 2019 Rachel Pope
Cover image © to Shutterstock.com

The author asserts the moral right to be identified as the author of this work.

No part of this publication may be reproduced, distributed, or transmitted in any form or by any means, including photocopying, recording, or other electronic or mechanical methods, without the prior written permission of the author, except in the case of brief quotations embodied in critical reviews and certain other non-commercial uses permitted by copyright law.

Requests for permission should be addressed to
Rachel Pope

ISBN - 978-0-6484884-3-9

Testimonies

"Rachel's ability to plumb the depths of grief and to unearth its sacred treasures is an inspiration and a joy. She navigates the darkness of this difficult subject with courage and grace, lighting a trail for others to find their way. This book is a gift to all who have bravely loved and lost."
Elizabeth Best ~ Author of *Eli's Wings* and *The Year We Seized the Day*

"Rachel literally walked through the valley of the shadow of death herself when she lost the three men she loved most in the world, her dad, her brother and then her husband and soulmate Ray. But, Rachel has come out of the darkness and into the light and with her carries gifts from that time that are too precious to keep to herself. In this book she shares the thoughts from the depths of her soul and the profound things she has learned through the journey of grief and loss. Through the process of healing she has learned the greatest gifts ever, empathy and the art of gratitude which in turn has carried her into a life of richness, purpose and HOPE that she never dreamed possible."
Kerrie Atherton, Founder of Stories of HOPE Australia - Author, Inspirational Speaker, Trauma and Addictions Recovery Coach/Counsellor/Educator

Dedicated to my Mum
Eileen Roberts
For she has never stopped believing, loving, and providing.
I owe it all to Her.

Acknowledgements

To my Family. More than any words can describe, I am forever grateful. My Mum Eileen, Bill, my special brothers Glen and Julian who have supported me along the way, Louise, Renee, Ryan, Liv, Larry, Sylvia, Kathy, Patrick, Olive, Val, Paul and all of my close relatives. Also to my beautiful new extended family John, Lesley, Melinda, Marco and Aleara. You are constant and kind. In your own special way, you have all played a part in my life and supported my children and me, through our toughest days. I consider you to be my lifeblood and nothing is more important to me than Family.

To my girlfriend sisters. There is no greater bond than a friendship that lasts a lifetime. No matter how far I've strayed, no matter how dark my days were, you were ALWAYS there for me. And to this day I will never forget the memories, the tears, the laughter and the adventures we have shared. Ange, Genevieve, Annmarie, Tarni, Michelle, Shar, and Kaz – I know you will always have my back. I love you so much.

To Jason, the amazing Man I get to experience life with now. It was written in the stars. You are my light, my rock, my laughter, and my forever more. You are beyond amazing in your loyalty, respect, understanding, and dedication to us as a family. You are a wonderful Father to our kids. Thank you for being ever so patient on this journey with me. I am so excited for the adventures that lay ahead for us.

To my gorgeous 'bonus' daughter Ella, I loved you from the moment I met you. Your smile lights up any room and your special gift is in understanding others and being there for people, a loyalty you get from your Dad. I am so blessed to have come into your life, at a time, that I've witnessed you grow into the beautiful young lady you are today. Keep being you.

To the incredible woman who brought these pages to life, Shilpa Agarwal. Thank you for your rock-steady patience and guidance throughout my book-writing journey. Your coaching and communication skills are first class. I have gained so much clarity from working with you and was gifted much more than bringing this book to the world. It was the hardest achievement I have ever undertaken, and you were there for me on every step of the way. A million thank you's.

To Kerrie and Eli for believing in me. I will be forever grateful for your constant guidance and encouragement. I am so proud to call such esteemed authors and mentors as my beautiful friends. To Paul and Guinevere for the many years of mentorship when I needed it the most, I am so thankful for your kindness and wisdom. To Craig Harper for kick-starting my confidence, helping me own up, and step up. To Toni for your creativity and igniting my vision.

Lastly, to the two people that have been the centre of my world, my driving force, and my reason for continuing to get back up again, for as long as I can remember.

My beautiful daughter Amelia Jean, and my mighty son Vincent Murray, one day you will understand why you are the very reason I am still standing. You literally saved my life. Why? Because you never gave up on me, you never complained, you always saw the good in every moment, even when your world was falling down around you. Your tiny hands held me, your laughter revived me, and your unconditional love rescued me. You have encouraged me to bring this book to life and I'm sure, also often wondered, why it was taking so long! The world is not big enough for your hearts and minds, but I sure do hope I live to see the wonders you create wherever you go. Your Daddy is beaming with pride from heaven watching you grow. He was so in awe of you both.

I am the luckiest person in the world that God chose me to be your Mum. I LOVE YOU with every inch of my being.

Xo Rachel

Introduction

"A day will come when the story inside you will want to breathe on its own. That's when you will start writing."
-Sarah Noffke

I have survived and I have surfaced. There will always be good days and bad days. My personal twenty-six-year grief journey has taught me many lessons. Sweet memories are woven from good times and I've learnt to seek beauty in the ordinary and magnify the magic.

Death is messy, and living with grief is hard. Nevertheless, LIFE is also messy and hard. I have come to realise it is our perspective that alters the happy and the sad. I am eternally grateful for the life I have forged behind me, life right NOW, and am excited for what lies ahead of me. This year I became immensely inspired to contribute in the narrative on the topic of grief. Over the years, I have personally witnessed the power of a story shared.

This is my story, and my twelve "Gifts From Grief". It is important to note that I believe there is no right or wrong way to grieve. Everyone's experiences are different. But I can tell you what has worked for me, what I've tried, and what I have learnt. Through my story, it is my wish to bring hope to many, and help others on their grief journey. Death and Grief will touch us all at one stage or another, and yet why is it the least talked about?! I'm lifting the lid on grief, one conversation at a time. If I could share MY one truth from my experiences and what I've learnt bedside to many last breaths, is that in the end, LOVE is ALL that matters.

Xo Rachel

Contents

Chapter 1
The Gift of Gratitude........................... 1

Chapter 2
The Gift of Growth............................ 13

Chapter 3
The Gift of Perspective 27

Chapter 4
The Gift of Compassion........................ 37

Chapter 5
The Gift of Resilience........................ 45

Chapter 6
The Gift of Vulnerability..................... 55

Chapter 7
The Gift of Love (amplified).................. 63

Chapter 8
The Gift of Spontaneity....................... 73

Chapter 9
The Gift of Purpose........................... 81

Chapter 10
The Gift of Contribution...................... 89

Chapter 11
The Gift of Adventure 97

Chapter 12
Gift of Empowerment (Wholehearted Living) 107

Chapter 13
Bonus Chapter: Let's Lift the Lid 117

A Mother's Arms

A Mother's Arms
Strong and warm,
A heart so full of love
Her body wears the proof,
They grow so fast
The memories so sweet,
Captured in her heart
From teaching those tiny feet.

Too many tears to count
Because you lost
Your Daddy too soon,
But those memories remain
Alongside a new love complete
A mother's arms.
She carries so much pride, joy, AND hurt
But one thing's for certain
Shell always put them first.

Rachel Pope

Gratitude

Makes sense of our past
Creates happiness in the present
And hope for our future

@giftsfromgrief

Chapter 1
The Gift of Gratitude

"Gratitude is the healthiest of all human emotions. The more you express gratitude for what you have, the more likely you'll have even more to express gratitude for."
–Zig Ziglar

What does gratitude actually mean? And how do you find gratitude in the bad times, as well as the good? In this chapter, we explore why the practice of daily gratitude is an essential part of the healing process during tough times. When we are blanketed by grief, it is important to find gratitude in the small moments, the little things that bring a smile to our face, and cling to that.

It took me a long time, twenty-five years actually, to come a full circle on my grief journey and feel grateful every day. Yes, every day, even in the trenches of life. Grief is complicated and it never ends. On the surface, Grief and Gratitude are unlikely passengers on the same train. But with time, healing, and a lot of growth, I've come to embrace the many gifts that have come my way. I have taught myself to find ways to practice gratitude daily. This has helped me heal immensely, and in return, I've been rewarded with a richer sense of purpose for my life.

In the early stages of grief, it's easy to be angry, bitter, and envious, play victim, asking that monster question "why me?" and "it's not fair!" This mindset can cause you to be stuck for a very long time. This is what happened to me. It wasn't until the last three to five years that

I've learned to turn that around. I know it seems like an unachievable task when recovering from a devastating loss, but I'm here to tell you it's doable, essential, and such a valuable asset, once taught.

There is no doubt that grief changes you. You see many things in a different light. I'm hoping that by sharing what I have learned from my experiences through compounded grief, you can take away some tools and strategies to help you move forward in a healthy more positive way.

Here are some questions that have come up regularly for me, not all the time but the reality is that they are still there, maybe you can relate.

"What have I to be grateful for, when so much bad stuff has happened?"

"How do I pick up the pieces, and live a normal life beyond loss?"

"How do I find joy again, when I'm constantly reminded of my loss, and feel sad because of the memories?"

I get asked these questions often. The truth is, I don't have all the answers. I am sharing authentically from my heart, in the hope that what I bring from my experiences can help others on their journey. No two grief journeys are the same, and I respect and honour yours. The gift of gratitude was chosen to be the first chapter as I truly believe it is the foundation of all healing. What I want for you the reader is the ability to OWN your grief because I want you to know that although I understand the heartache, the loss, and the pain, I can't give you all the answers. No one can. You have to face it, allow it, honour it, and not wish for it to go away. What I CAN do is offer hope that there will be good days, in fact, great days, if you learn to manage the many peaks and troughs along the way.

By bringing awareness to the gift of gratitude, we can recognise the joy in the small things. It can be the start of something really beautiful, when we learn to open our hearts and minds to what is around us, in the here and now. Once noticed, then other good things flow into your life. If we are constantly focused on the negative, then guess what? We will only see more negative. Who knows that when we are thinking about buying a particular car, then all we see on the road are more of that make and model? Before the thought of purchasing that car, we didn't notice them at all. The same goes for our general thoughts of positivity verse negativity. If we fill our minds with negative thought patterns and input, then all we will see in people and situations around us is the bad stuff. We will quickly learn to not see the good in people or moments.

I've become so much more aware by learning the art of practicing gratitude, and I value that gift from my grief experiences. I value the growth, and the much fuller life I have embraced despite my loss. So rather than fixating on what I'm missing and what has happened to me, I can learn to stop, watch, and live each moment. Don't get me wrong, the pain of losing someone, and a piece of your heart, never goes away. You'll always miss them. Not a day goes by when I don't think about the people in my life I have lost. Nevertheless, I truly believe in the lessons their legacies have taught me, providing me with gifts I would never have gained, if not for the experience. I now focus on the good memories, that make me smile or laugh when I think of them, and slowly, the pain of the loss does not take up so much room in my heart. Which in turn, has allowed more joy and good times to take grief's place.

If you learn to embrace gratitude and find joy in YOUR life, it doesn't mean you're trying to brush your loss under the carpet or you're trying to ignore it. It means that, with time, you can learn to grow through your grief and find a way to live your best life. Don't you think that's what your loved ones would want for you?

So what does it mean to be grateful in grief? Well, for many who haven't experienced a loss or great loss, it may be easy to practice some form of gratefulness daily. I have a good life, I have a wonderful family, I have a good job, etc. It's relatively easy when things are smooth sailing. On the other hand, you may have been gifted this awareness through your grief, and you never really practiced any gratitude before your loss. We are all guilty of cruising through life not giving thanks when all is going well. If you are quite happy moving through the ups and downs of life not really knowing what gratitude is, then even better to put this into practice before you need it the most.

Widowed at 38 years old, I was faced with a decision. Do I dive down that rabbit hole of victimhood and self-pity once more, as I did at a young age with the loss of my Dad, or do I pick myself up and start on a journey deep within? A mission to find all that I could to be grateful for in my new life, as is right now, as a solo parent.

When you have two small children to feed, dress, and get out of the house, you are forced to wake up and face each day. They did save me, there is no doubt in that. I had the blessing of my beautiful children to teach me how to live in the moment. There is a beautiful rainbow drawing made by my daughter Amelia at the time her daddy was gravely ill. It has a flower growing underneath the rainbow, bathed in rays of sunshine and reminds me of her view on the world in spite of what was going on around her. Even with everything she witnessed, all the hospital visits, the countless strangers in and out of our home, the tears and anxiety as she sat by me, despite all the emotional and irregular turmoil she must have felt at an age where kids desire routine and security, Amelia still saw life, light and colours in her little six-year-old world.

Kids are very good at living in the moment, aren't they?

And in witnessing that, I was able to get up each morning and recognise the joy in the small moments. For me, everything was amplified. Every smell, sound and sight. The smell of freshly baked cookies, the sound of the kids laughing in the bath, the beautiful image of their long lashes asleep at night. At that moment, I knew my life had changed forever, not just in circumstance, but in my new found perspective on the world around me.

I could go to bed every night with a grateful heart, but to be raw and honest, the difficult part was waking up. That was when I opened my eyes to see the empty side of the bed. The mornings were the hardest, as I was reminded every morning of my loss as soon as I opened my eyes. That side of the bed was empty. He was never coming back. The love of my life, the man I met when I was just 22 years old, the father of my children, had departed this earth way too soon. Each morning I would think to myself "I'm not going to make it", "I don't have the strength to get through this". The nightmare was real. But then the little moments would creep into my day. Reminders of LIFE, good deeds by people I loved, songs and laughter from the children I taught, the ocean and its beauty. It was these little signs that slowly birthed my new perspective of gratitude and growth through grief.

I knew it was the beginning of a whole new world. Although I didn't choose to be navigating, I knew from that moment on, I had a daily decision to make. I could lay down and be a dormant mother, or I could rise up and be the best version of me possible, despite what I was going through. I didn't see the growth then, but years later, I can honestly look back and be so proud of how far I've come. Most of all, be proud of the example I was setting for my kids. Never give up.

I certainly did not have this perspective when I lost my Dad at the tender age of 17, nor the awareness of personal growth. I was angry and bitter. When your whole world has been turned upside down at such a young age, you are not equipped with any higher perspective or growth mindset. When my Dad passed away, I was suddenly faced with not just missing my dad and the memories of our past, but I also had to grieve all of the things I was going to miss out on in the future.

Milestones like eighteenth and twenty-first birthdays, and later weddings, all were tainted with bittersweet tears. Having to be with your friends while their Dads took the stage to say how proud they were of their sons and daughters, it was really hard to not be bitter in those moments. It was like a dagger through my heart.

In those young selfish years, I definitely felt like the victim, that life was not fair, and questioned life and all its meaning.

Now that I have come a full circle, I have a deeper sense of gratitude for having such an amazing father. I can look back and say how lucky I was to have such a present and wonderful Dad. Some people don't have that in their lives, and you don't see it at the time. My Dad Brian, was a kind man of integrity and honour. He never put anyone down or spoke poorly of a single soul. He was an encourager, a true gentleman. He made people feel loved, important and had such a warm beautiful heart.

Some fond memories of mine were following him around in the dark making him coffee before his early golf games. I remember learning to water ski on the front of his skis with special little footholds on his. I remember falling asleep in his lap in front of the TV, and when I got too big for that, I would kneel beside his chair and put my head on the armrest and he would play with my hair. I remember the proud days he took me to work as a little girl. I remember my Dad asking my Mum to dance at a wedding, then going around and asking all the other ladies as well to make them feel special.

I hope I leave my kids with those memories, the small moments. They are the ones that count. The cuddles and encouragement, the way I make people feel loved, that's how I want to be remembered. It really is a great reminder to us all to learn to slow down, to create and cherish the small moments, amongst the rush of life.

It wasn't until I lost my husband that I had that insight. I had to take myself back and let go of some really painful memories around the time of my Dad's death. It took a long time to bundle up all the grief of what I was missing out on, and turn it into a bundle of gratitude for everything that I was fortunate to have had, growing up with such an incredible Father. It's those memories that I now hold on to the most. Every now and again the nightmares of watching a strong Man, your idol and King, fade away to a skeleton of a man (The wretched horror of Cancer), will creep back in. Nonetheless, they are further apart now, I guess that has come with time, and so many more good memories to fill my heart.

All the things that I've learned during my grief to gratitude journey have been life-changing, for the better. I now possess the gift of seeing things differently. I take time to create memories because I know I can't get that time back. When you practice gratitude daily, you become a lot more spontaneous and intuitively more aware. You take more photos of your loved ones because you realize how important pictures are. That only comes from experiencing the pain of one day realising the pictures are all you have left.

I am more grateful for the people in my life now. I am instinctively more respectful and grateful for the elderly, and the special stories and wisdom they have to share because I don't have my grandparents anymore. If you are blessed to still have your elderly parents or grandparents around, I encourage you to share and record some stories of theirs. Your future family will thank you.

Gratitude simply turns what we have into enough. You can't change your past, you cannot control the future. So why not choose joy in the present, right now because no one is guaranteed tomorrow. Gratitude unlocks the fullness of life. It allows us to live in the present moment without wasting time wishing for the things we don't have or wanting a different past. There's just no point. It is better to learn to be happy with what you have in the existing moment and accept it as enough. It's just part of your journey, and you are where you are for a reason. It will be a catalyst for attracting more happiness into your life. It will prompt you and propel you forward in a positive way. I'm not here to say that it's easy though. I know it is hard drowning in grief to be hopeful for a better future. I'm just here as an example, a living proof that a full life can be enjoyed alongside your grief. It's not healthy to stay stuck in a cloud of sadness with no anticipation for the future.

I think there is also a lesson for people not in grief, or for people helping someone who is grieving. The Gift of Gratitude is one of the greatest gifts of all. I can put a hand on my heart say, that each morning when I open my eyes, I am thankful for another day. Thankful that I received the gift of a day. At night I crawl in and say thank you for my bed and everybody around me, but I also thank in advance for things that haven't happened yet. Here's the kicker, I also give thanks for my hardships and for all the crap! It is an art to practice gratitude on an ongoing basis as your new normal, but I can vouch for the way it changes your emotional state. If you choose to be positive, then you can trick our brain and lift yourself out of the sadness that you're going through when you're grieving.

Don't get me wrong, it's not all sunshine and rainbows over my head. I'm sharing this because I've seen it all. I know what real pain is, I know the darkness of death. I've had to sit and tell my 4 and 6-year-old that their Daddy is gone, and won't ever be coming back. I know I can't take away your pain, no one can, but I am passionate about helping people through the process.

There definitely have been a few weeks during this book-writing experience where I've had to take a step back, and allow myself to feel that pain all over again. It was just another reminder. Grief was overpowering my other emotions, so the clear message is, neither the grief will go away nor can you hide it or fake it that it's not there. It is very important to acknowledge grief. You can't push it back.

I guess that's an educational part of the book, which I want people to know that it's okay to not be okay, and it's okay to have those dark days. I used to call them "doona days" where I would drop my kids at school and I would crawl back to bed the whole day because I just didn't want to face the world. And the next day, I would get up again and I'd start over. So, it's okay to have those days and rest or ring somebody to talk about it. Just don't stay there, the next day and the day after, soaked in grief, years later it'll still be there. Acknowledging grief as an emotion, I believe, is one of the biggest things we can teach through our experiences to help others. It is also vital that we allow these conversations to be had without fear of judgement, or misunderstanding, or helplessness. When you hear other people's stories it presents another opportunity to be grateful for what you have now.

I'm hoping to lift the lid on the conversations around grief to educate people that it doesn't go away, it's not something you get over. We need to be comfortable when talking about that, we need to say their name, we need to not make it a taboo and have people uncomfortable talking about their loved ones, that's all part of the process.

Recognising the gift of gratitude only came to me years later, having experienced so much loss in my life. That gratitude leads to love in more ways than one, and it's now my foundation to all things. The art of living with gratitude starts with learning to take care of yourself and appreciate the beauty and strength within you. If I hadn't maintained that attitude of gratitude, my life would be completely different; I would have felt sorry for myself all the time, forever, as a victim. It's taken me a long time to be aware of that. In those early years of losing my dad, and my brother, I didn't have the awareness, and if I hadn't lost my husband I don't think I would have grown so much to develop a deep sense of gratitude in all things. I have my children, Amelia and Vincent, to be thankful for teaching me that ultimate gift.

As we move through these gifts in the following chapters, my wish for you is to recognise and value your own Gifts from Grief. To honour and celebrate the survivor in you. The holder of the memories, the one who carries a piece of your loved ones' heart, forever in yours. At the end of the book, there is a bonus chapter with some space to write your own thoughts and ideas for growth. Let's work through this together.

***

> **SMILE OFTEN, BE THANKFUL, AND LOVE WHOLEHEARTEDLY**
>
> –Xo Rachel

Hello Grief.
I know you.
I also know me.
I'm not the same person.
I will sit with you.
But I will also grow through you.
I accept you.
But my heart has expanded,
and there is room for more,
than just you.

@giftsfromgrief

Chapter 2
The Gift of Growth

"When you experience unimaginable loss, you won't ever be the same person again. A new self will emerge, gifted from that grief."
–Xo Rachel

I clearly remember waking up one day, one year after the devastating loss of my Husband, and realising how much not only my world as I knew it had changed but that I had changed. I was not the same person, in every way. Personal growth, as a by-product from experiencing loss, can be embraced or it can be fought. I can now acknowledge my inner work and transformational growth throughout my grief journey, and be proud of who I've become because of it.

With every loss that I've had in my life, I've gone through some kind of transformation, whether that be good or bad, positive or negative, it's all considered growth. It wasn't until I was faced with widowhood, as a young mother, that I was truly thrown on a rollercoaster of personal growth, and one that I could not avoid. I was faced with many inward, contemplative questions like "Who am I now? Where does my true identity lie now that a part of me is missing? What are MY core values?"

I'm a different person now with different dreams and goals. I had to sit with that and question my values, my internal shifts and, as a solo parent, create my own dreams and goals that, we no longer shared, as you do in a marriage. This, I hope, can be relatable not just through the loss of a spouse, but also loss of a parent, and your identity as a daughter or son. Child loss, and your identity as their primary caregiver. Pregnancy loss and attaching your identity with being a parent. OR all grief, I believe encompasses some kind of identity loss.

So I had to ask myself - "How can I grow to be a better and stronger person?" "How can I still grieve, in a healthier way than I had done before?" and still be moving forward. It was really a huge turning point in my life because I recognised I hadn't allowed that to happen with the loss of my Dad and Brother. I hadn't allowed myself that time to grieve and grow. I had fought it, pushed it under the carpet. I didn't know that grief was an emotion that was meant to be felt. I did not know that it was okay for it to never end and that there were ways I could embrace the growth.

I made a decision then and there that I wasn't going to lie down and slowly watch my entire life in me be sucked away with the tide. I had two beautiful children who were my entire world, and I vowed to be more than just a "survival" role-model to them, someone who not only overcomes but also finds joy again, no matter what.

It's hard to grieve and be in the middle of that, and not lose yourself along the way or lose it altogether! There was definitely a period of time where I was stuck in my grief, often two steps forward and three steps back. Not knowing myself at all, not being able to imagine ever being happy again, not being able to project what my life would look like in five, ten or fifteen years' time. There truly is a time in early grief where you are operating in survival mode, but slowly, if you allow it, a new stronger self will emerge.

This did not happen overnight for me. Actually, it wasn't until I hit rock bottom, then clawed my way back, one baby step at a time and allowed myself time to breathe. I looked back and realised I had never talked about this. I've never spoken about how I survived. The loss of my husband resurfaced all the hurt, anger, and anxiety from losing my Dad and my Brother. I realised there is something missing here; I wanted to grieve all over again, but not with pain in my heart, rather with love and memories, and laughter, appreciation and gratitude. I realised how much I had GROWN in my grief this time around.

I quickly learnt that I not only was drowning in sorrow for my beloved Ray but also reliving the heartbreaking losses from all those years ago. It truly was a full circle.

The growth, I recognised, was how far I had actually travelled personally, things that I had achieved in my life, and all the obstacles I had overcome that reside with living with loss every day. The light bulb moment of acknowledging my own personal growth, and being proud of that, is really what drove me to study grief and the human experience more. So how can we help each other through this time? How can we accept the growth? How can we be kind to ourselves through the process? And how can we learn to grow through our grief?

No one escapes grief, grief does not discriminate, and I am so passionate about opening up those conversations around it so that people don't get stuck. I know it to be true to spend years stuck in those early grief stages, by that I mean, not moving forward at all, to any steps toward healing. I want to give people hope, strategies and insights into my own journey so that we can support each other along the way, without judgment.

I want to express clearly here, there is no right or wrong way. I am not here to tell anyone how to grieve or put any time frames on healing. It's your journey and you own it. I do, however, want to encourage a life of joy and happiness beyond loss, that there are ways we can embrace our grief and still feel the pain, learn to acknowledge it, feel it, and yet still celebrate new joys.

"Life is too short to miss making memories."
-Xo Rachel

I am an example to people to know they can be living a fuller life. I want to shift our mindset from a "grief stage" to a "getting over it stage" and then to a "living again stage". I'm here to help and share another way. A way to live in sync with all the above, the grief troughs alongside the life highs, AND the moving forward, not the getting over. Because in my humble opinion, there's no such thing as getting OVER grief.

How do we deal with it? How do we help others through it? And how can we learn from each other?

I think it's that saying: "It's only from rock bottom that you can rebuild yourself." And I think it took all that stripping back for myself to realise - when you're faced with losing your life partner, you lose your identity along the way. I developed an awareness of growth through my mistakes as well as my wins. It is all part of the growth process, and it's only now that I can recognise it as a gift because I've learned so much in the last six years. That is what led me to write this book.

I did get lost for a while. I found myself questioning my purpose. I sold my business, I was trying to raise two small children, full of fears of the future and what it might hold. I had to learn to start all over again. It was definitely a journey of self-discovery, one I didn't know would lead me to give back, knowing in my heart I could use this growth for good. I found myself asking, "What is the purpose of the loss?" I knew I was still standing for a reason and that's when I finally accepted the journey and made the decision "I'm going to turn this around."

I decided this is their gift to me, for a better life moving forward. I know a lot of people will find that hard to swallow. How can my life be better off without my loved one? And for others, just the thought of future loss can leave us paralysed with fear. So when I talked about gratitude in the first chapter as being a primary gift, from my grief, it is to teach people how to live that "now", before the inevitable loss. To appreciate what is in front of us already and be grateful for that. That way there are fewer regrets and sadness for the inevitable, whenever that time comes for all of us. Wouldn't it be a wonderful world, if we took the time each day to appreciate fully the people and goodness in our lives?

It made me question myself, "Are some people blessed to travel through most of their life without losing a loved one until quite late in life? IS that lucky or not? Or do they miss this precious gift of a new perspective and gratitude to live more fully and present?" For me, I am now able to be grateful for every day I live, grateful for everyone around me, and with each loss, I've grown. So, there are many lessons I've learned along the way.

It's not something I wish upon anyone, but I do wish my perspective on life to others sometimes. It's all our own journey to be experienced. I can remember people saying to me, post-loss, "You're so strong; I don't know how you do it; I could never do what you do." Well, I didn't ask for it. I was running a business, I was teaching, turning up singing and smiling to my early learning classes, and then back home to a four and six-year-old with usual parenting duties. The truth is, under the cover of darkness, when the kids went to bed, **I didn't feel strong at all.** So people were seeing me as this strong person, but the reality was, I was terrified and weak in spirit. I was exhausted, floundering, angry and scared to pieces. There's no strength in those emotions. It's the journey of the grieving soul.

Looking back now I can see where my true strength lay. I still had to get out of bed the next day, and there is strength in that. I held a job down, running my business, I turned up with cupcakes for class birthday parties, and managed to volunteer here and there. I kept my kids alive, there's strength in that!

So if you're not feeling too strong in your grieving journey, know that sometimes your strength is just in the showing up. That when people tell you how strong you are, maybe they're just recognising how you look okay, and that you're managing to smile, you're turning up for work, you're keeping yourself and children alive. They don't know what else to say because they can't FEEL your pain, but they do recognise your strength in just getting by. I wish I could go back and gently tell my thirty-eight-year old self that

"Maybe you don't have to move mountains or miraculously recover overnight from a devastating loss to find the strength within you, sometimes it's just in the simple daily tasks done with peace, compassion and care for yourself and your family... that to me is the real strength."

-Xo Rachel

Because of my personal gift of growth, I hope to shed light on a society which holds expectations on those experiencing the pain of life after loss. Gosh, we give people one day off to go to a funeral and expect them to turn up the next day as if life is completely back to normal. We need more support and education surrounding grief, in our communities, workplaces and schools. Most of all, we need to talk about it.

There's a real thing such as 'grief fog', you really can't concentrate for very long periods at a time and it can show up physically in many ways: memory loss and focus and other physical symptoms. Just getting through daily tasks can be a huge effect on people who are grieving. That can go on for a very long time. It could be months or years for people who don't reach out and get some help, to take some practical steps to overcome all sorts of physical and mental by-products of grief. I learnt this the hard way. We are going to cover "How to help" and 'Things to say" in our bonus chapter. So how was life after loss, as a widow you might be wondering?

Looking back, the initial year was one of survival mode; I was just going through the motions. I was very blessed to have family support and my children were surrounded by love. And this is where I want to educate people who are friends of someone who is grieving. It's not often in the first year that we have to monitor closely the well-being of someone who has experienced heartbreaking loss. It's in the next year, and the year after that, we really should be checking in. This is the danger zone for friends or family who may feel like "You should be over this by now", or they simply don't want to talk about it for fear of "triggering you". This is where grief can resurface like a tsunami because it seems like everyone else has moved on with their lives and the grieving person is still left with the daily reminders of their loss, especially as a solo parent. Couple that with the pressure we put on ourselves to be healed and recovered from our loss, it can be a very crippling and lonely time.

I have had friends who have shared with me similar experiences when it comes to pregnancy, still-birth or infant loss. They have openly shared that it is was as though no one wants to acknowledge it over time, for the fear of "bringing it up". They have also said that some people truly believe it shouldn't be affecting them (parents of pregnancy or infant loss) as much as if it was some other kind of loss. This breaks my heart. Because of the community, I have grown, I have learnt so much about life after this kind of devastating loss, and how unsupported a lot of parents feel. Always, always ask. The grieving person will most likely tell you kindly if they are not in the frame of mind to talk about it, but better to say "I don't know what to say" than to say nothing at all.

Remember, acknowledging grief is the first step to helping people heal and move forward in a healthy way. Notice how I keep referring to "moving forward" and never "moving on".

Initially, we often look for outside fixes to fill that hole, when you have time and finally breathe, "I'm a year on. What does life hold for me now?' More often we can be catapulted into replacing our sadness or that gap with quick fixes, alcohol, shopping, mindless scrolling, a holiday- definitely nothing wrong with a holiday, it can be something to take your mind off. What I was talking about (quick fixes) is the avoidance of facing the grief itself, the fear of having to face yourself. I can remember wanting desperately to move house because I wanted a new environment, I didn't want to be there any more in the house that Ray had just passed away in, there were just too many memories, and that can be different for everybody and for some people they want to hold on to that.

For me, I was willing to let go of all the material stuff because Ray wasn't in the house, he was in my heart. And his memories were not dependent on the house that we were living in. I told myself, Ray's memories will move with us and just by giving my body, my mind a newer environment, it would help me in my healing journey. The growth came from being brave, from stepping outside my comfort zone, and for listening to my heart.

I wasn't leaving a support network; for some people that would be harder. I do remember some people telling me it was too soon, and that it was a rushed decision, I should hold on to the house and things like that. But I knew in my heart that I needed to have a sea change.

So, that's exactly what we did and I packed up the kids and bought a unit by the sea. That was the best decision I ever made because it just allowed a new sense of adventure to colour our world, and we cover the "gift of adventure" in chapter eleven. The gift of courage and the gift of adventure. That sea change allowed us to receive that.

So, I encourage you to take a look at some external quick fixes that may be filling your void. Speaking from experience, being very vulnerable and truthful about it, there was alcohol or food or shopping or dating for me to try and push down the emotions. The growth came when I was gifted with the awareness that those things did not serve me anymore. Luckily, it came before any negative effects on my life. Let's not wait until that happens on larger financial or health scare stage. The reality was that I had to learn some lessons in self-care, and to fall in love again but with ME first. I started with myself and that was the best thing that I could do for my kids and for myself. From that was to slowly heal and discover new goals for myself. Becoming your own cheerleader is hard when you've had that unconditionally in a loving marriage. Your partner or parent are the ones that support you and encourage you to try new things or to challenge yourself. They are the first people you call when you are celebrating a win, but also the ones you call when things go pear-shaped. You have to learn to do that for yourself and that's a huge gift because not a lot of people can do that. Learning to back yourself is another part of the growth process.

There are many gifts of growth. What I want to do is to help people learn some baby steps to grow *through their grief* rather than *being stuck in their grief.* It could be as simple as moving your body each day or going through a walk in nature. Baby steps because that brings a positive change in the mindset. Taking care of yourself and surrounding yourself with positivity through reading and listening, filling your mind with positive so that there's no room for negativity. Playing music, little tips you can do to put yourself in a positive mindset to get through the day.

The first thing do is to trust the process. Trust yourself that everything's going to develop and happen at the time just right for you. Try not got compare your grief journey with anyone else's, and ignore anyone's well-meaning advice to tell you that you should be over it now or you should be in a different space now, you should be meeting new people now - that's just all different for every single person. There's no right or wrong way and the acknowledgement and trust in the process that you are going to grow from this is where the gift begins to unwrap itself.

You may not recognize it at the time, a few years down the track you will look back and realize how far you've come. Set small goals for yourself, like just getting through one week at a time or in the day I used to say, "If you've managed a shower and a sandwich, then celebrate it as a good day."

There's something profound in just the simple act of stopping and taking stock of how far we've come. I think we put too much pressure on ourselves to achieve so much rather than allowing us to evolve through the process.

Honour your grief
Just like having a newborn baby, when your role is just to care for them and take care of yourself, there's nothing beyond that in those early days. I think we look too far ahead. Especially when you're widowed young, you are often faced with questioning your future and projecting yourself in about ten years' time, how will I cope? What if I can't cope with work? What if I don't meet anyone ever again? What if I am a solo mum for the rest of my life? How is this is going to affect my children? How am I going to provide for them emotionally and financially? These were all hard-hitting questions and fears I held heavy on my heart.

Learning to take a moment to be present in the "now", and recognize that with each day, with each baby step, you are gaining more strength within yourself. Be willing to embrace the changes and not get overwhelmed with the future, even though you didn't want the change. I know you didn't ask for it but taught myself to look at the opportunity in the changes. Soon enough I started to notice the things that wouldn't have come about if that tragedy had not happened in my life.

It is in that process you will rediscover your strengths and a whole new skill set that you would never have taken on. This is part of unwrapping the gift of perspective we dive into in chapter three. As I approach the seventh anniversary of Ray's passing this year in 2019, I recognize I am still growing, evolving, constantly learning around my grief. The most important aspect is accepting and sitting with it, not allowing it to consume me and knowing that it does not define who I am.

I'm so grateful for the growth. If I didn't experience that loss, I wouldn't have discovered so much about myself. I'm not saying it in a selfish way, just that how else do you make sense of it all? What is the alternative? To stay stuck. To stay forever depressed, angry, and alone. By changing my mindset to one of gratitude and positivity it has allowed me to be a better person, a better parent, and partner etc. Let's lift the lid on these gifts together and encourage each other in the process. There is an unhealthy stigma surrounding time frames and expectations for people to move on. We should not feel ashamed in our grieving process even if it's ten, fifteen years down the track.

Let's make it okay to not be okay and teach and help each other by example that there are happy moments to be had, new memories to be treated and new adventures to be had, despite our loss.

We still need to live a full life.
I want you to embrace the duality of being sad and happy at the same time. There are still going to be painful memories, you are still going to miss them daily. If we trust and accept that the grieving doesn't go away, but learn better coping mechanisms and healthy ways to enjoy life again, we can teach a whole new generation about life and loss. I'm proud that I feel confident in sharing this. I'm not ashamed to speak about it as I think we live in a stunted society when it comes to grief.

Finally, recognise that there's strength in just getting back up again. Be kind on yourself through the growth. Don't have huge expectations, and learn to trust your inner intuition again. Take the time to stop and be present. That's where the strength and the growth come from. It comes from just doing things you never imagined yourself doing, or pushing yourself through things you thought you couldn't do. We all have that capability within us.

※ ※ ※

"DON'T WAIT FOR THE LIGHT AT THE END OF THE TUNNEL; YOU HAVE TO STOP AND LIGHT THE TORCH FOR YOURSELF."

–Xo Rachel

life is **GOOD**
life **IS** good
LIFE is good

@giftsfromgrief

Chapter 3
The Gift of Perspective

"How lucky I am to have something that makes saying goodbye so hard"
-Winnie the Pooh

I've learnt that two people can look at the exact same thing and see something totally different. I've also learnt that the only thing you sometimes have control over is perspective.

*"Life is **GOOD**, life **IS** good, **LIFE** is good"* I created this quote to represent the different seasons I've travelled through on my personal grief journey. There were times when all I could be grateful for was the very fact that I was still alive, and would simply open my eyes in the morning to say, "Well, at least I'm still standing and my kids still have a mother." I.e. "**LIFE** is good"

There were other times when my faith would be so tested questioning "Why is there so much pain and suffering in the world?" "Why do good people die young?" And then something magical would happen. Life would deliver me a snippet of pure joy to remind me "Life **IS** good" if I choose to recognise these moments with simple gratitude.

The beauty in my new gift of perspective is that these moments would then lead to seeking more moments. Learning to magnify the magic. These are the heart and soul ones. The ones that truly make you feel alive. The adventure, the spirit, the love, the world and all its beauty. These are the memories that create the perspective of believing "Life is **GOOD**"!

I'm sure you agree, grief can deliver all three perspectives in one day. In this chapter, we're going to talk about how we can learn from each other in our grieving process, if we take the time to put things into perspective, in a more positive way. I have discovered that it really is a gift when you learn to acknowledge and harness the power of how you look at life and death. I haven't spoken to a single person who hasn't had a shift in perspective having experienced grief and unimaginable loss. Death of a loved one automatically changes your perspective on things, and it's hard to put that across to others who haven't walked in your shoes.

I must add here that I certainly haven't always carried this healthy dose of perspective in life after loss. As a teenager, for many years after the death of my Dad, I was bitter, lost and angry with the world. You could ask yourself the question "Am I holding on to un-resourceful emotions?" Stuck with a victim-like perspective of "Bad things always happen to me," or "Everyone else is lucky".

It took many years for me to realise that staying stuck in this "victim" mode was not serving me at all. What I learnt was that carrying the underdog story around on my chest was holding me back in many ways. It was actually stopping me from truly living again.

I guess I gained my first dose of perspective quite young. I was born in Brisbane in 1974, the youngest to three older brothers. My parents Brian and Eileen were hard working and gave us every opportunity in life. One of my earliest memories is swinging off the parallel bars that they built for my brother to practice walking, with callipers attached to his legs. My eldest brother Brett was born with Neuroblastoma tumour on his spine, that was discovered in infancy which led to a series of operations and lengthy hospitals stays during his first years of life.

Therapies, further operations and radiation treatment saw Brett in and out of the hospital for months, and a year at a time, with my incredible Mum home-schooling him in between, trying to send him to normal schools to give him a sense of inclusion. As he grew, his spine continued to curve and a further serious operation paralysed him from his waist down. This meant he was to spend the rest of his life in a wheelchair. My parents were incredible teachers and did everything in their power to allow Brett to live an adventurous life, despite his disability. Because of that Brett achieved the many opportunities to be involved in sporting competitions and travels around the world. By doing so, they raised a very independent and high achieving human being.

We grew up with a "no barriers perspective and a sense of empathy toward others who faced struggles. I have our parents to thank for that. I can always tell when I meet a young person today if they have a sibling or parent with any kind of special needs. They just have an aura of compassion toward others and maturity beyond their years.

A healthy perspective on life despite circumstance was combined with the resilience and strength that our parent's gained as they fought against all odds to give my brother a normal life. On top of that was a deep sense of gratitude, a by-product of our upbringing. We appreciated the little things. We helped others and we looked beyond appearances to not judge people by the way they looked.

My childhood was full of happy memories of camping, holidays and water skiing. Later in life, Brett went on to achieve amazing things; he competed in Pacific disabled games in London as a teenager, the Commonwealth Games in Australia competing in several sports winning many medals along the way. He competed in table tennis, swimming, track events and basketball. Brett went on to do a University degree in psychology. He gave himself to others by volunteering on a crisis hotline and lifeline work. He did ground-breaking work for Qantas airlines, researching disabled travel. Truly, he did live his life to the max, as best as he could, even at times whilst facing unimaginable obstacles and pain, discrimination and daily struggles as simple as finding a car park.

All of that amazing living life to the max. All that fighting. All that endurance and painful operations and everyday struggles. All of that adventure that sent him to live in other countries and explore the world. All of that helping others with a great sense of purpose and surviving all odds. All of that came to a devastating end, on 5th February 2000.

I was to receive a phone call in the middle of the night that will never leave me.

"There's been a car accident", then I heard the words, through sobs "Brett is gone."

I just remembered crouching down in the dark, thinking this is a crazy nightmare. This only happens in movies. I wanted to scream, I was immediately transported back to the grief of losing my Dad once more, wishing this whole tragedy to go away. How much can one family bear? 'Here we go again, this can't be happening to us.'

Anyone who has lost someone young, to grow angel wings often questions "Why do amazing men and women die far too young?" We've all heard the song "only the good die young". A few years earlier I had been dealt with another tragedy, when a young man, John, I had dated, died instantly in a car accident. He was an old soul and I truly believe people like him and my brother were sent to us as teachers. The irony is that John's circle of friends led me to meet my husband Ray. The beautiful lessons they leave the world, deliver us a healthy dose of perspective. We as human beings have to decide whether to accept or ignore the lessons. I certainly have carried them right through my life. When you lose someone you can't replace, it makes you aware of how much we attach ourselves and our identity to things. Houses, cars, clothes, jobs, status, they all CAN be replaced. One of the biggest gifts from grief is the awareness that none of these externals truly matter when bedside to someone taking their last breath.

When you've been gifted this perspective, even though you carry the pain as well, life looks a whole lot different. For me, it was for the better, in the long run. More unwrapping of these gifts later. Brett's story is a testimony on having a perspective on life. He was sent to us to teach us that.

In this chapter, I want to help people put their grief into perspective. To see how they can learn and grow, while still allowing the grief to flow. One of the biggest lessons I had to learn, as a young widow, Mother, and business owner was the ability to embrace these lessons. Let's explore them.

1. Give yourself permission to slow down.

2. Teach yourself the ability to constantly ask some effective questions as exampled below:

"What is my present state better than?"
"Could my present state be worse?"

3. I want us to explore how to swipe the victim mentality once and for all, learning to embrace life beyond loss. The one you've been gifted. You are not defined by your loss. I was Fatherless, I had lost a sibling, a boyfriend, and widowed, but I do not define myself as a WIDOW.

Let's dive into these a little more
1. **Give yourself permission to slow down:** In this tech age of instant gratification and answers, I think sometimes we might get impatient with the grieving process too. And not allowing ourselves time, we want everything to be okay in an instant. We want our kids to be okay, and we want our situation and our finances to be okay. On top of that, our well-meaning family and friends want to fix our pain in an instant as well because they hate seeing us hurt so much. However, grieving takes time, and if it's talked about, we can recognize that it's a journey, there's no beginning and no end to grief. One of the simplest ways to gain perspective on your changed life is to give yourself permission to sit with your grief, even if that means facing the pain sometimes. I know it sounds simple, but I'll often remind myself to take a moment to slow down. Try this with your breathing, with your talking, walking, listening, eating, loving, giving, and taking.

Slow down because in a moment, this moment will be gone and some moments you get a chance to repeat and others you may not, so slow down. You may discover new things and discover what you've found.

2. **Ask yourself some effective questions.** "What is my present state better than?" I can mourn the past of what I'm missing, my Dad, and those moments lost, and I can also mourn the future. Those

memories will never get created. Nonetheless, if spend too much time there, I could be missing out on what is right in front of me. My present state is actually a wonderful life filled with new memories, new experiences, and I have so much to be grateful for.

Our young children are the greatest teachers of this. They don't miss out on opportunities for joy because they're not worrying about what to cook for dinner, what is about to happen, or what has happened a week ago. They live in the present moment and don't need reminding that they are not promised tomorrow. If there is fun to be had they'll dive right in. It is always important, I feel, to open their eyes to the world around them and educate them on the way other people live. When we took our first family holiday post-loss, to where my brother and his family were living in Fiji, it was a great opportunity for this.

My children were able to gain a broader view of their privileges, their comforts and how fortunate they were as young children living in Australia. We were there for Christmas so it was a good opportunity to make grateful lists, like clean water, electricity, schools, an abundance of food and everyday luxuries. I'm forever glad that we gave them this experience. So another good perspective question to ask yourself is "Could it have been worse?" Well, the answer is always yes to that. You only have to turn on the news to see multiple tragedies and losses others face.

I believe that's where the gift of compassion and empathy comes in.

I'm not saying to compare your losses or problems with somebody else, but we can look at the world around us and find another person's circumstances we would not be willing to swap with.

When we ask ourselves some of these perspective questions we can adopt a new view of "life IS good"; life, in general, is good. The alternative is not so inviting to me. I want to live, I want to live a good life. I want it to be filled with happy memories amongst the chaos, and it's up to me to create them. That is a perspective you gain with grief because you just appreciate life in its purest forms.

Those who are grieving would understand why I cry at the simplest of things… the puppy commercial, the Father's day clip, a newborn baby, a happy movie ending.

When we slow down and take time to appreciate the little things, life is good, we will experience more joy than pain. Sometimes we just don't allow ourselves the time to take a moment to be aware of the beauty in front of us. We hold on to the pain more than we do with good memories. One tool I use is to consciously take my mind to a happy place when I'm questioning my perspective on life, or when I'm feeling like a victim of circumstance, or overwhelmed and I just can't seem to see the light. You can teach yourself how to light that torch for yourself and gain some new perspective on your current feelings.

3. Lastly, let's explore the idea of living with a "Victim mentality", in the sense that you will always see life as unfair. It is upholding a belief that bad things will always happen to you, and others are to blame for our misfortunes. In a sense, I did carry that for many years after my Dad died. Followed by subsequent compounded loss and grief, I believed I was cursed. I told myself nothing good happens to our family. That life is unfair and cruel. To harbour this for too long would mean I would take on the belief that everything is out of my control. In fact, it can become a habitual way of looking at life, not allowing that healthy perspective to grow beyond your loss.

The good news is that it is a learned, acquired behaviour and we can undo it when we learn to see things in that perspective. Practising gratitude etc. like we talked about in chapter one. Even though I lost at such a young age, I still had much to be grateful for. However, if I didn't flip that switch, nothing would have changed in my eyes, and I would not have gained a new perspective. I would have been playing the victim, miserable for the rest of my life. There was a lesson in that for me. The way we embrace life in the face of death. In the end, I don't wish my circumstances on anyone, but I do wish my perspective on life to them sometimes. These are just some ways I've dealt with my grief and those hard-hitting questions.

One thing we can all do is talk more about it. Maybe that will help more people understand and accept that death is a part of life, and none of us will escape the grief road. Let's not brush it under the carpet. Embrace your new perspective. And how you show up for yourself and the people around you as someone who's embraced this new perspective or someone who's down with the victim mentality. By accepting it as a gift and taking ownership, you can move from being stuck to being a superpower.

* * *

> **I WISH I COULD HELP YOU SEE, LITTLE MOMENTS ARE IN FACT THE BIG MEMORIES. AND WHAT YOU THINK MATTERS MOST, DOES NOT MATTER AT ALL.**
>
> **–Xo Rachel**

she has a gift for
compassion
for she has seen
too much
for one heart to
bear

@giftsfromgrief

Chapter 4
The Gift of Compassion

"Compassion is a nurtured gift to look beyond your own pain, to see the pain of those others."
-Xo Rachel

There is something unique about a person who has been through many trials and challenges. You know when you meet someone and just have an intuition that they have a story behind their smile. There is an air of understanding, grace and compassion. They are the ones who offer kind gestures when others are thinking of themselves. These kind gestures, from someone who has walked in your shoes, can help others in ways that only compassion can heal.

Compassion is an action word. It has no boundaries. I believe it is one of the most powerful forces in the world. What we often forget is that for this to spread throughout the world we also have to learn their art of self-compassion, which I will touch on here too.

Within a short time of losing my husband, I found myself helping out in one way or another, all across my community. I don't feel I deliberately sought it out, different situations just presented themselves to me. I guess the gift of recognising the need to help others was born from receiving help myself in the past.

I know now, my gift of purpose is to help those grieving and especially when I hear of someone young being widowed, my heart just breaks.

The memories of those early days flood me, and I am compelled to reach out to them because I know what's ahead of them. The blessing I didn't count on was what it did to my own personal healing. What I quickly learnt was that there is no better exercise for a grieving heart than that of helping others. Yes, there were times when I was weary, but something drew me to get up and do it anyway.

> *"The best way to not feel hopeless is to get up and do something. Don't wait for good things to happen to you. If you go out and make some good things happen, you fill the world with hope, you will fill yourself with hope"*
> **-Barack Obama**

It is certainly the last words of this quote that resonated with me the most. Getting out of the bed and helping others was a really positive way to fill my own heart with hope, in a time when I needed to find it the most.

As I navigated my way through the many long roads and valleys after my loss, I came to realise that compassion is something we grow into, and is not readily acquired. I do feel my upbringing, as the youngest of three older brothers with my eldest brother Brett having a disability, that a dose of compassion was nurtured in us at a young age. I have come to learn that my challenges and grief journey have become the most valuable learning resources for me.

Having awareness of life's little hidden messages within every situation, good or bad, allows us a better chance at deciphering the gift within the grief.

Let's look at some keys to bring some awareness to your own gift of compassion. If we lift the lid on your own understanding of what it means to be compassionate, despite your circumstances, then I hope that it might help you move forward in your grief.

Number one: Find a cause or a way to volunteer and help, with some of your time, somebody else.

Number two: Be a listening ear in your area to connect with people who have gone through loss.

Number Three: Turn that compassion toward yourself.

How do we do that?

Step one: When we offer some time to volunteer there is a guaranteed release of good endorphins.
The year after my Husband passed away was our son's first year at school; he had just turned 5. I was still running an early learning franchise but wanted to keep an eye on him, and his well-being during the first part of his big year. Yes, my volunteering in his class was coming from a need of my own, initially, but I had Mondays off and cleared the morning to help out in any way I could.

Did I feel like doing it? Most days no, I didn't really have the energy to put on the brave face with people who knew us as a family. Initially, I volunteered to be by his side, but what came from it was a deep sense of pride and well-being. It gave me a sense of purpose and took my mind off my situation. The big bonus was that it allowed my son to see me coping, helping others and setting an example of what it means to give.

Here are some examples of organizations you might know of, to nurture your gift of compassion from your loss. Local charity thrift shops, cooking kitchens, local libraries, schools, or hospitals. The simple act of donating clothes and items is another good way to help others while helping yourself. There's plenty of organizations out there that can do with extra help in the form of your time. You might not feel qualified, but I want to remind you that you are qualified because of what you have been through. And by doing so, your own heart will expand. It's important to listen to your own intuition with where you spend your time to help and find something that connects with your soul but is easy on your heart. I.e. you may not be ready to volunteer in circles that bring up too much pain with your own situation. Trust that the right things will come to you. Another by-product of volunteering is the strength and growth that comes from putting yourself outside your comfort zone.

Remember to do only as much as you can. It could be one hour a week, or even one hour per month.

Step two: Be a listening ear in your local community, in meet-ups or online network circles and try to connect.
Have you ever heard someone else's story and thought, "This is exactly what I needed to hear today?" I want to encourage you that YOUR story will do that for someone else. I know the sense of relief when I tell someone my story and they reply with understanding because they've been through a similar one or know someone who has. Sometimes it can be hard to talk to friends when maybe you might feel they just don't understand what you're going through. By finding groups or other people that do understand, you can connect in a way that is helpful to everyone. I know grief can be a very lonely journey when you feel like you have no one to talk to, there are always ways to connect with other people on a similar journey as you.

Look for connect-groups in your area, even business meet-ups are valuable as there is always a personal connection involved when you find someone you connect with. I know it can feel right outside your comfort zone but for me, I was surprised with how many friends I have made. What I also found was that automatically I saw I was a little further along in my grieve journey than somebody else. You know, it might bring up some things for you versus grief journey alone. It may help someone else because they can see how far you've come. Your compassion for their situation will shine through and give them a little hope.

Step three: This very important component of compassion nurturing is to learn to turn that compassion towards yourself.
But first, we must love ourselves.

Self-compassion goes beyond what we think of as just self-care. It means that we learn to be less hard on ourselves. It means that we accept our mistakes, learn from them and move on. If your compassion does not include yourself, you will be giving from an empty vessel. When you nurture yourself with the same kindness and love that you give to others, everyone benefits.

That means taking care of immediate needs but also lifting heavy expectations off yourself. Know that you are doing the best you can with what you have. Compassion is all things of the heart - sympathy, emotions, empathy, understanding, concern, and kindness. So if we are in tune and on purpose to give that to others, we can see why these are important traits to show ourselves.

Let's ask ourselves, how can I give myself an experience of any of those feelings and words listed above? How can I show some understanding towards myself and be kind to me, even when we have those bad days? To be compassionate and proud of how far you've come. That might mean making a purposeful cup of tea each day, doing a class or joining a group, beginning to exercise, or just investing that time to be compassionate towards yourself. A lot of you know how much harder those days are, in your grief, if we have the added burden of being hard on ourselves.

The gift of compassion is also recognising that you still have the capacity to give even when going through a hard time. In fact, it is often because of these circumstances that draw us to give back. It's not our place to tell people what they should or should not be doing post-loss. Just the very practice of giving and showing compassion toward others and their circumstances will allow shifts in your own mindset and the grieving process.

***

“KINDNESS IS A LANGUAGE THE DEAF CAN HEAR AND THE BLIND CAN SEE”

–Mark Twain

strength
comes from pushing
through the things
you thought you couldn't

@giftsfromgrief

Chapter 5
The Gift of Resilience

"Never give up. There is no such thing as an ending, just a new beginning."
-Xo Rachel

Have you ever wondered how some people are able to cope so well with difficult circumstances, and others at times, fall in a heap at the smallest of challenges? Many times in my life I have been told that I've been dealt an "unlucky" hand when it comes to personal loss. Well, this was a truth/story I told myself for a long time. A while ago, I unlearned this story and started to tell myself a new one.

Yes, it is true that I have experienced hard things. I have seen tragic, heartbreaking scenes that I cannot "un-see". These will stay with me for life. Do I call that unlucky now? The answer is 'No' because I now tell myself a new truth/story.

The story about my lucky gift, in fact, sometimes I see it as a superpower! I have direct access to a well of resilience that lives in the very core of my being. It has seen me in good stead through many challenges in my adult life, and I also know that my children draw on their inner resilience too. A "never give up" that attitude. A resilient mindset, I hope will assist them through almost any situation life throws their way. I have been able to nurture and develop this gift of resilience because of my own personal growth through loss and grief. It has enabled me, for the most part, to cope with the most trying situations.

I believe we are all born with this gift within us, however, most of us are not aware of how to harness it.

What is true resilience?

Christian Moore in his work resilliencebreakthrough.com states, "Becoming resilient starts with the realisation that the diversity we experience in pain, discrimination or challenge, can be converted to a powerful fuel that can actually bring opportunity." He talks about the great lessons in the power of resilience and what it means to jump back up when life literally has you on your knees.

There are many benefits to recognising and drawing on that inner resilience within yourself. When it comes to grief and loss, we are automatically thrown into a do or die tunnel. Get up or lay down. How we react to certain situations is a measure of how much resilience we are drawing on. We must recognise it as a wonderful gift from grief.

I quickly discovered my inner resilience after the loss of my Dad at such a young age. Facing the many challenges, two months into my flight training, I had to get up each morning and face the world regardless of how I was feeling. I had to dig deep, overcome an array of fears and not think about death when I had just experienced a life-changing loss for the first time.

Flight or fright mode certainly takes on a new perspective when you are literally learning to fly an aircraft! And I was just seventeen! When you are forced to flip the switch to operation mode, you quickly learn not to bring any rollercoaster of emotions into your training. I was a good pilot, a good student, and passed all my flight tests. How did I do that when I was hurting so badly on the inside? I can only put it down to that innate desire to do well, to push ourselves beyond what we think we are capable of. I must add though that I was in a very supportive and nurturing environment, with a loving family and friends propping me up. I can certainly see how, when facing devastating loss or challenges, if not supported in a caring and favourable environment, could lead to a downward spiral. Don't get me wrong, I did go off the rails quite a few times, like a lot of teenagers do, crashing through the barriers of learning and young adulthood. Nevertheless, I always returned to the love that my Mum and friends surrounded me with.

So this brings me to the gift. Now, when I'm faced with fears or situations where I'm required to flip the switch on my thinking, I take a moment to reset, remember and reshape my thoughts. This ignites my inner resilience and allows me to face a situation in a way that is resourceful, not damaging. It is also important to take the time to stop and remind ourselves of our own personal achievements and over-comings.

You are a tremendous being, capable of great things and you have overcome hard stuff before. There is no reason why you can't do it again!

There are many places I take my mind to when required to reset my thought patterns. One of them is my first-night solo flight in my late teens, in a Cessna 172. For those who don't know, that's a relatively small single engine, high-fixed winged four-seater aircraft that holds about 21 gallons (79 litres) of fuel in each tank with a top speed of about 302km/hr. Let me describe the feeling of flying 6000 ft. above the ground on a perfectly clear night. The town lights twinkle like Christmas tree lights. The hum of the small engine is incredibly loud when you are the only thing up there! I'll never forget that night from Brisbane to Bundaberg, which is about a three-hour trip. Without showing my age, I had no GPS navigation system, and no mobile phone. I was actually flying with a little night light, a pen-light torch in my mouth, a map on my lap, and the basic aircraft instrument systems. I will just never forget that surreal moment because it was so clear and for a minute, I could just forget all my worries, mesmerised by the lights across the horizon.

I look back now and realise how much resilience I was drawing on at that moment. Just so much courage and strength, for me having been through what I'd been through, I really don't know how I did it. Now I know we all have this resilience inside us, and I was just going through the motions. We've all heard that action cures fear and I just had to do it, I had no choice. When you're up in the sky, you can't decide "I don't want to do this anymore," you have to land safely and get home. One thing is for sure, I'll never forget that euphoric feeling when I touched down at my destination. I had such an overwhelming feeling of achievement and pride. When you face something like that, your fears, that's where resilience keeps building and building. I can remember crying and crying all the way home because that was for me and my Dad! I also woke to the fact that he wasn't going to be there for me to share many more stories like that. All I could hold on to was the comfort of knowing he was with me the whole time and got me through it. This is a time in my life that I take myself to, often, to draw on my resilience to overcome many challenging situations.

I tell myself - if I can get through that, then I can get through anything now. What is something you've forgotten about from your past that was an example of you using your resilience and strength to overcome?

In this chapter, we recognize this ability to cope in such situations. What will help us along the way as we grow through our grief? It is certainly something I've been very mindful in fostering for my kids as well. What I want to cover here are some keys to nurturing your own inner resilience, through life after loss.

1. In each moment of challenge ask yourself, "How can I stop in this present moment and flip my thinking?"
2. Let's look at ways to lift the grief cloud you might have hovering over your head when you're trying to break through barriers of emotional heaviness and pain.
3. Strategies for accepting and acknowledging that life doesn't get easier or more forgiving, we get stronger. By doing so, we bare the circumstances and become more resilient.

So how do we do that?

Step 1: In each moment of challenge ask yourself, "How can I stop in this present moment and flip my thinking?"
We all have a choice in each moment. I can dwell on the past, and the root of our thoughts often comes from our past, I can worry about the future and what might happen and spend time out there. Or I can be present right here at this moment. I can ground myself with breathing,

bring myself out of my head and into my body, and allow myself to act in the present moment. I.e. not a moment from my past, or a moment that hasn't happened yet. Can you see the difference?

This is a really effective way to catch yourself. I even have post-it notes in my car to remind myself to breathe. It seems simple and people think it is, but when was the last time you actually took some really mindful deep breaths? It can flip your thinking to move forward and make a more positive decision based on that. So how do we flip that thinking? I know it's hard in the moments of grief, where you're reminded of fears, fears of the future, or fears of what's happening in your life now. Memories, emotions and waves of overwhelm. I get it.

I love Mel Robbins and her 5-second rule. The elements of the 5-second rule (melrobbins.com) are a very effective way to trick the brain to stop overthinking.

"When you feel yourself hesitate before doing something that you know you should do, count 5-4-3-2-1-GO and move towards action.

There is a window that exists between the moment you have an instinct to change and your mind killing it. It's a 5-second window. And it exists for everyone. If you do not take action on your instinct to change, you will stay stagnant. You will not change." `-Mel Robbins

The lesson in it is that we often spend too much time in our head. So, when the alarm goes off in the morning, you've got five seconds to get up and get moving. If you hit the snooze button and roll over or spend too much time worrying about your day, then you've lost that first positive moment in starting your day. And the same applies to fear and grief. I know for me when I spent too much time worrying about my kids, as a young widow, I could overthink the heck out of scenarios that had not happened yet. If I had allowed myself to stay there, I would not have let them out of my sight. It was easy to stop at that moment, count backwards from 5 to GO - action. By doing this, I was putting positivity into my head to say, "Nothing is going to happen to them, it's okay, we're going to do what we are about to do, and that's going to help them rather than holding them back."

Step two: Ways to lift the grief cloud and break through those barriers of emotional heaviness and pain.
The emotional heaviness that comes from grief is well known to those who have experienced loss. I describe them as those heavy X-ray blankets you get at the dentist. I know for years I felt it was one blanket on and then it would come off a year later, then two blankets back on, and so on. This is a great physical heaviness on your chest. And there were times when I thought that it was always going to stay that way. In this step, I want to talk about the positive ways to lift this heaviness. That these blankets don't have to cloud your entire day. Yes, you are still going to have those heavy days, and grief is guaranteed to come and go in waves. My hope is that you will equip yourself with some ways to cope with the heaviness without it weighing your whole self down, one layer at a time.

I realize how much grief I allowed to build up inside of me. It wasn't until I lost my husband and I looked back and realized how much I had let the grief of losing my dad and my brother gather so much heaviness and pain. I wasn't equipped to lift those blankets on my own, and one thing is for sure, it can quickly become toxic to your health, relationships with others and yourself. If you don't allow yourself to grow through your grief and recognize the resilience in you, you will not move forward.

Step three: Ways of acknowledging and accepting that life doesn't get easier or more forgiving, we get stronger. By doing so, I can better my circumstances and become more resilient.
We're all going to face heartache and grief at some stage, we need to accept that it doesn't discriminate - nobody gets away from experiencing that in life. We need to accept and acknowledge that. We can compare ourselves to others sometimes and take on the bitter end of the stick, but the truth is everybody is going through something in their lives. Someone else challenges may be a breeze to someone else, but that does make it easier for the person who is challenged. Knowing and accepting our own challenges as just that they are "our own", we can become more resilient to facing them. We only get one shot at life, and I don't want to get to the end and have more regrets in my life than good memories. So I can focus on the grief, or I can accept it as PART

of my story. Not the WHOLE story! My chapters are not finished yet, I have so much living to do.

So how can we learn to live a joyful life, when some days there won't be anything to be joyful about? I could have easily thrown in the towel at the very beginning of my flying career, after losing my beloved Dad, but I would have missed out on all that growth, knowledge, and adventure. I can also look at the gifts of resilience at such a young age now. It gave me such an opportunity to grow from that. And you can grow through your grief and gain this amazing human superpower along the way. Resilience is accepting your new reality even if it's not the most desirable one or worse than your reality before. It is realising that you can choose to flip your thinking. You can choose, at that moment, to be happy anyway despite your circumstance. There is always light somewhere if you take the time to search for it.

***

"I AM NOT WHAT HAPPENED TO ME, I AM WHAT I CHOOSE TO BECOME"

–Carl Gustav Jung

Staying **vulnerable** is a risk we have to take if we want to experience **connection**
- *brené brown*

@giftsfromgrief

Chapter 6
The Gift of Vulnerability

"What makes you vulnerable makes you beautiful."
−Brene Brown

Sharing my story, when I talk about the gift of vulnerability, is really a true reflection of my own vulnerability. For the last 12 months, I'm constantly reminded of how far I've come. Writing this book has meant that I've been brave enough to reveal all the ugly with the good as well as the gifts. For me also, staying vulnerable means I recognise how far I've got to go if I'm going to continue to help others. There's no holding back. I used to worry about offending people, or making people feel awkward by bringing up my whole life story again or telling too much. Nevertheless, I think it's imperative to let people know that they are not alone in their journey. I realised that If my story was to help others then it needed to be the whole truth. The good, the bad and the ugly. I wanted to share my triumphs, alongside my lows. To me, vulnerability is courage, and it equals connection. Sometimes it means speaking the truth even if it hurts because it is in that releasing of the heart that I found where the true healing begins. The blessing comes when your vulnerability helps others. This is my passion and purpose for sharing.

In the book 'Daring Greatly', it is shared that being vulnerable transforms the way we live, love, parent and lead. By Dr Brene Brown, vulnerability is described as uncertainty, risk and emotional exposure. Brene states that vulnerability is the birthplace of love, belonging, joy, courage, empathy and creativity. And I think there are many benefits to nurturing that vulnerable side. Often in our society, we're taught that vulnerability equates weakness, fear, or hurt and we associate it with all that heavy stuff we want to avoid; all the emotions we sweep under the carpet. And I'm here to tell you that in the last few years, I've exposed more personal vulnerability than ever before, and the benefits of that have been many.

In my story, it wasn't until I was faced with life as a young widowed mum that my vulnerability was magnified tenfold. I had a choice and I could either hide allowing those blankets of grief to pile on me again like after my dad and brother died or I could start stripping back all the layers and reveal it all. This is how I ended up here, writing this. I realized that there was nothing wrong with me. Being vulnerable in those early years after I lost my husband, I hated asking for help, like I'm not good enough. I was always meant to be the person who is the giver. I spent 18 months as a caretaker playing many roles simultaneously – that of a nurse, mother, business owner, and nursing my husband through a year of chemo and everything that goes along with that. Where I've had ways and helpers and family and friends advise, I had to be very vulnerable to step outside of myself and ask for help and to get that help from people.

At times, there's also that vulnerability of feeling the pressure to have gotten over it by now, to have moved on and been strong years later. We tend to hide our vulnerability for the fear of being seen weak. Often as grievers, we won't show that side or won't let the vulnerability come out. That can result in a lack of support in not asking for help. Basically, what I want to talk about is allowing our vulnerability to come up to the surface for the many benefits it has. That it's okay to be scared, and being scared often means that you're about to do something really, really brave. As a widow, I needed to acknowledge the brave steps that I had already taken myself and also allow the vulnerability to be a sign of growth. This is because if you allow this to the surface then there's a whole new world of learning and acceptance of ourselves and of others.

So how do we embrace vulnerability as a gift from grief? Let's talk about how we can embrace vulnerability.

Step one: be courageous.
So let's look at what it means to be courageous.

Number one, our greatest potential lies beyond the safe side. Number two, have you ever wondered how vulnerable should I let myself be? Where do I draw the line? There's no standard for this. You have to play in your vulnerable zone and find your own boundaries and zone of growth. And if 'vulnerability' is the highest form of courage, what are we talking about when we talk about courage? Courage is having strength in the face of pain or grief. Courage is the ability to act on one's beliefs without the fear of disapproval. You might resonate with courage in some other words that can be daring or being bold, and grit, to grit or gallantry among other things. But when we talk about courage in vulnerability, it means letting your guard down. It means showing people you're not perfect and don't have it all together. It means that you can be your own perfect self with us and that they can grow, they can let their guard down, and it means that they can relax a bit.

So let's dig a bit deeper on how you can you be courageous and embrace all the emotions that are showing up for you right now. One way to do that is to give affirmations. And I invite you to look at some affirmations around courage. I'll share with you a few that I used and that helped me as reminders for myself. One of them is

'I am enough'. And that just means that wherever you are at this moment in your grieving journey, you are enough. *'My courage is stronger than my fear'*, *'I am a survivor'*, *'I have the strength and resilience to grow through my grief'*. These are just a few affirmations I use daily. Now, I invite you to choose your own favourite descriptive words and advice that empower you with your mood and give you hope, which in turn will develop your courage.

Step two: Open up more. That's another step nurturing our vulnerability. Why should we open up? It's a catch 22 with vulnerability. If we protect ourselves to avoid getting hurt or because we fear what people may think, then yes, we avoid those feelings, but we miss out on much more. We miss out on the true connection.

I truly believe that it's through sharing the stories of the good and bad that allow people to feel less alone. And if we do avoid it and if we do protect ourselves, then we also subconsciously teach ourselves that these feelings need to be avoided. So we are not teaching the right things to our children either. What I want to cover here is that the sort of opening to either acceptance or rejection is scary. I want to share how I did it and how I helped myself and in turn helped other people in their grieving journey. I think the best way we can do that, how we can do that and open up is to talk, talk, and talk. Find a safe space – be it with a group, grief group or friend or a therapist, and tell your story by writing it down or by speaking it out. We need to let it out, all the ugly bits where you feel you are in your grief process, whether it be one month, six months, five, ten years down the track, regardless of how uncomfortable you think people may feel. Opening up these conversations around grief is so needed in our society where people can't read minds.

How do we know if our friends and family are doing okay in their grief journey? It is hard in a society that sees vulnerability as a weakness. I can see how mental health is a huge, huge issue because people don't want to show that vulnerable side. I know that when we see that vulnerable side in our partners, we feel so deeply for them and the connection and intimacy grow between the two people on a whole new level. If our kids see that in us too, it's such an invaluable gift to them. I know part of my kid's healthy healing after losing their Dad has a lot to do with them seeing that vulnerability in me. Knowing that it's okay to not be okay some days. That it's okay to talk about it, to talk about fears and things like that, and so that now I can look back, and if one of my children are overwhelmed or having a bad week, then I can say to them that it's okay and remember that we all get overwhelmed sometimes. I can talk about it from experience and they can recognize that in me. When our kids see that it's okay to lose it, but in doing so, teach them healthy ways to do that without harming or lashing out on anyone else. This is one of the biggest gifts to them. I can say, "Mummy is really sad today because…" Or "I'm really sorry I am short of patience today, but this is what happened, or what I'm feeling," then we bear down and hug tight, and you're teaching your kids to show their feelings as well by showing your vulnerable side.

There are many benefits to opening up. So let's lift the lid and open up the conversations on how you can help your friends as well after recognizing that they're going through this vulnerable stage. It might be hard for them to admit they are not okay at times, they may feel the pressure to get over it by now if significant time has passed. So it's just... recognizing it might be hard for them to open up and share that they are in their grief journey because they fear what people may think. They fear being seen as weak. I know for me, the first time I shared my full story when I spoke at an event Stories of Hope Australia (stroiesofhope.com.au), I had planned to get up and be this pillar of positive strength and deliver my uplifting speech to about 80 people in the room. I ended up reading the entire speech from behind the podium. I was so nervous and anxious and had all physical symptoms of bearing your vulnerability with anxiety; tightness in the chest, and just wanting to run away. Nonetheless, what I did I was courageous in all that mess of vulnerability.

What I realized is that it allowed so many people to connect with me, after the number of messages I received from people saying that they related to what I presented. I think if I had stood up and delivered that perfectly polished piece, then the outcome would have been different. People like seeing the vulnerability in others because it allows them to open up as well.

So you can support your grieving friend with the gift of vulnerability by lending a patient ear to them. Just let them talk if they need to talk. It is important to make them feel comfortable to ask for help.

I used to think that I had to have fully recovered and healed in my grief before I could help others. That I had to have no more anxiety or problems attached to my grieving journey. That I had to be a picture of positivity to help others. Now I realize by having the courage to reveal my vulnerable side, I have so much more power to help many others in their grief journey.

**

> **LOSS AND HEARTACHE ARE NOT WHO YOU ARE, THEY ARE PART OF YOUR STORY**
>
> **–Xo Rachel**

LOVE
is the desire to
GIVE
not to receive

@giftsfromgrief

Chapter 7
The Gift of Love
(amplified)

"Grief, I've learned, is really just love. It's all the love you want to give but cannot. All that unspent love gathers up in the corners of your eyes, the lump in your throat, and in that hollow part of your chest. Grief is just love with no place to go."

-Jamie Anderson

This was so paramount in my early 'post-loss' years. The transformation came four years on. The day I met Him. The Man that came after. My love Jason, and his beautiful daughter Ella, who have turned our tight little world of three into five, plus one adorable furry companion Ralph. Jason was the one who turned the lump in my throat to laughter, my tears into sweet joys. My kid's empty spaces into a full house of fun. The hollow part of my chest was still there, but the rest of my heart expanded. There was suddenly room for so much more. The bonus was that I didn't know I was capable of so much more love when I had lost it all before. You see, I had thought I would never be able to love again. I believed in happy ever after. Guess what, I still have my happy ever after. If we are still living and breathing, then as human beings, we are deserving of happiness, to love and to be loved, and very, very capable of complex emotions.

The surprise for many is that the love comes back intensified and amplified because we know what it is like to lose it. It's that whole renewal of gratitude and perspective again. There is no taking someone for granted. There is no time wasted.

My desire for this chapter is for you to embrace the gift of amplified love. When you feel so deeply about everything on your grief journey, you have every right to be riding an emotional roller-coaster because you have experienced the deep pain of loss and therefore that means you have once loved greatly. Sometimes you might think that your heart is so broken that it will never mend, nor be able to love again. And why I want to share my love story is because I want to give you hope. I'm sharing this chapter because I want you to know that your broken pieces are beautiful and just like a magical puzzle, they all fit together into one great masterpiece. Some days you'll feel like you're missing so many of the pieces and other days you'll fall upon fresh eyes to help your pieces together, the bigger picture. With that comes amplified love.

It is perfectly normal to think that you'll never love the same way again when your heart has been shattered to a million pieces because of the heartbreaking loss. But what if I told you that in growing through your grief, your heart actually expands. In fact, I found that the people who have lost are the ones who possess this beautiful quality of love amplified, knowing that you are still going through your grief and you will experience a happy heart again. I think the world needs more people who love deeply, not less. Because I had experienced so much heartache, I had to learn to live and love on a whole new level and everything was amplified, even the songs, movies and commercials had me in tears. The Father's day commercials, newborn babies, life, death and everything in between gets permanently locked in your love radar. It can be exhausting at times, as you become super sensitive, but with that, you also become super loving. You hold on to your loved ones extra tight, you hope more, and you say I love you often.

There lies the gift in that. The loving more deeply is when you're open to expanding your heart and move in that direction of expansion rather than holding on to the heaviness and brokenness. Only then will you be ready to experience love amplified or a whole new adventure.

My 'second chance at love' story is still growing, and I love my guy more and more each day. It's not easy being the man who followed another lifetime and marriage. Blended families come with challenges that we are navigating and learning with each moment. Love is the answer to all the little problems, and we both have experienced so much happiness in building a new life together. I'm forever grateful that I met someone who has accepted us with patience and understanding of our situation. The kids and I talk about their Dad when the moments present themselves and we still honour his birthdays and special anniversaries.

It was the gift of adventure, the gift of (self) Compassion and the gift of Growth that I believe allowed my heat to be fully able to receive and give "all in", truly ready to give and receive love again. I do believe everything is meant to happen at the right time. Before that, I had thought I was ready and dated, but it was all part of the journey, navigating me through the maze of growth and new beginnings. I won't go much into dating after widowhood; there are lots of blogs online that address the ups and downs of this season. I can certainly say that it takes guts, it takes faith, it takes hope, it takes all the strength inviting that back into your life. All because you're aware of losing it all again. Was I scared? Yes. Was my new partner scared? Yes. Being a partner to a widow comes with its own challenges. But Jason has this beautiful quality of just being so authentic and real. And the kids are living in the present and have so much love to give because that's all they have ever known.

When faced with challenges and doubts, we gently remind each other that what we have is all brand new. If you're reading this and questioning whether it is all possible that you don't know how you can give your heart to someone else while still honouring what 'was', I'm here to give you hope. It is possible and we are very capable as human beings to carry this task. I want you to know that it's okay to love what 'was' and to love what 'is' now. You can still love your lost person, and enjoy a fulfilled life of love after. It is tough we navigate now, in our new life as a blended family, we'll always be reminded of our past with anniversaries and birthdays etc. But you find what works for you. I'm very lucky that I have found someone who honours my children's memory of their Daddy Ray and embraces the role of being their Dad here on earth while we remember their Dad in heaven. True Love... it's messy and beautiful all at once.

When I talk about the gift of amplified love I know this for sure that Jason recognized it straight away. It may sound familiar that we carry that gift of amplified love in our hearts because we are always so grateful. I appreciate my partner tenfold, we write each other notes and it's all those little things we speak several times a day because he knows that's important to me. But he also knows I'm super anxious at times and worry too much; that comes with the grieving heart. We're getting better each day, growing together, and we are so excited about our future that we have never looked back.

So what do we mean by the gift of amplified love? My definition of amplified love comes from a personal journey when I realized that grief changes you, that you become someone who loves more deeply but hurts more often. Love more openly and appreciate love greatly in all forms. Not just talking about romantic love but motherly love, sibling love, friendships, grandparents. I want to share some key points on how we can learn to live, laugh and love again after loss.

Step one: never be afraid to love deeply.

Step two: accept your sensitivity and emotional awareness as a new gift, not a flaw.

Step three: always remember the key to being able to love unconditionally comes first from loving yourself fully.

So let's look at step one: never be afraid to love deeply.

I've quoted here from the AMP Bible, Amplified Bible Corinthians 13:4-8 "For love endures with patience and serenity, love is kind and thoughtful, love bears all things, believes all things, hopes all things and endures all things." Anyone who has nursed a loved one through the brutal truth of cancer to the very end certainly knows this kind of amplified love. It was an 18-month journey nursing Ray through chemo and the roller-coaster of emotions that come with that. Staying positive and still managing to hold the whole family together at the same time.

I think that's where my gift of amplified love began to flourish. When you're nursing somebody, everything gets put aside and I guess a part of me has also been that way from watching my mum care for my brother Brett who spent a lot of his early years in and out of hospitals living life as a paraplegic, my older brothers and I would help with all that too. I think you can always tell the characteristics in someone who has had a child or a sibling with special needs growing up, they carry that empathy, compassion and genuine love for all people.

So what do we truly mean to love deeply? I think, some of those points, I don't believe it's a sign of weakness to wear your heart on your sleeve. Or to bring all the extra emotions to the table because your amplified love is a gift.

To love unconditionally is a difficult thing. It means there are no expectations to set. It means loving from the core of one's heart and living to give, not to receive. So how do we not be afraid of loving deeply again? Keep doing what you do best without fear and keep reminding yourself that you have so much love to give. Whoever is going to be on the receiving end of that, is a lucky person. Know that your gift of loving deeply is unique, beautiful and powerful.

If you were to embrace this as a gift, how would you open your heart to new connections, friends, family and dating? Just be proud, be kind, be you. Always remember your loved one would want you to receive the love you deserve. That they would want you to be happy and experience joy again. If you're still stuck under that heavy grief blanket, picture your loved one in the same room giving a hug. They would be so sad to see you crying all the time. It's time to pick yourself up and honour them by choosing joy.

Step two: accept and redirect your sensitivity and emotional awareness. Why? It's okay to be super sensitive, to cry more often and hope more desperately. In fact, it's perfectly normal for those who are grieving. Never apologise for being sensitive or emotional. Accept it as the gift of the big heart. Be proud that you are not afraid to let the world know. Showing your emotions is a sign of strength. It's usual for those who are grieving to experience a roller-coaster of emotions all in one day. If we don't learn to accept this new internal radar, it can get us worn out and over-anxious over anything and everything. Sometimes they can take everything too personally because of our sensitivity. So, we need to learn how to redirect it and bring awareness to it.

Being sensitive and empathetic towards others is a lost art in today's world. The digital connection has replaced true heart connection face-to-face. Being sensitive is not a flaw, it's not a sign of weakness, and you care deeply because you've seen death. You've been through hell. If we re-channel and turn that into a positive characteristic, you become passionate about life and that's contagious. People will be drawn to you because of your outlook at life and your ability to love so deeply. So how do we turn into a positive being knowing that it will help yourself and others? You need to know to redirect that emotional sensitivity awareness towards yourself as well, embrace each season; accept that this is who you are and you live in the present. With growth and time, these feelings of being sensitive and over emotional may change.

Know that your current season of grief will not stay the same in six months, two years, five years; you'll have grown and changed and you'll learn to live laugh and love again.

Step three: always remember, the key to be able to love unconditionally comes from being able to love yourself fully first.

> *"But first we must love ourselves"*
> **-Xo Rachel**

One of the most painful parts of losing a loved one is losing yourself in the process. As a widow, it may be hard and confronting to look in the mirror and see yourself without your other half cheering you. There also may be guilt and shame attached to your grieving about lost times, those things you never achieved together. With parent loss, you face the loss of support of your mum or dad who always believed in you no matter what. After losing a parent, rebuilding takes time, and we must let go of the lies in our head. You got to be okay on your own before you can be okay with someone else.

This part of the chapter is all about learning to love yourself again so that you'll be ready to receive love. In this section, we will cover a few things which you should always remember in the process of learning to love yourself all over again. How do we do that? The more you accept and love your current life (remember the chapter on gratitude) the more the life will love you back. Practice self-care; baby steps will lead you in the right direction of self-love.

Make decisions on what you want your life to look in the future, not hanging on to what has already passed. Two books I highly recommend for self-care and self-love are "Healthy Healing" by Michelle Steinke-Baumgard from One Fit Widow, and "The Art of Self Love" by Kim Morrison. It's important to love yourself enough to know that you're worth waiting for that special person to come into your life. Be patient, everything is coming together. Surround yourself with uplifting people. Sometimes it's not healthy to be in grief groups if it doesn't prompt you to move forward in a positive way. It can be depressing and you'll know when to leave those support groups, and find what works for you best.

* * *

I love this quote from Michelle Steinke-Baumgard from One Fit Widow.

> **"I DON'T WANT YOU TO SAVE ME, I WANT YOU TO STAND BY MY SIDE AS I SAVE MYSELF."**
>
> **–Michelle Steinke-Baumgard**

The best thing about
memories
is making new ones.

@giftsfromgrief

Chapter 8
The Gift of Spontaneity

"If you think adventure is dangerous, try routine; it's lethal"
–Paulo Coelho

It can be said that spontaneous people make the best of every situation they face, and take every opportunity to live life fully in any given moment. It can give you some great qualities to deal with whatever happens next. Spontaneity is a wonderful gift from grief to nurture. As someone who is grieving, you know all too well the fragility of life and therefore know not to let moments pass you by. Because of my grief journey, I have developed a new sense of adventure, more on that later, and also made more of a conscious effort to be more spontaneous.

Have you ever felt so stuck in your daily routine that you are just going through the motions? This can also be magnified in grief because we often have to switch to the survival mode just to get through the day. An example of that is feeling like you will never experience fun and joy again because you are living with this heavy grief in your heart. I know, for me, the years that followed Ray's passing were suddenly operating in survival mode. I owned and operated a GymbaROO franchise that began each day by setting up the equipment at 7:00 AM, which also meant bringing my seven and nine-year-olds with me full-time. Mornings were interesting. Then, at night, after dinner, it was about reading books and tucking-in, I would walk out and look at the dish chairs, and think to myself "do dishes or emails?" Whichever would win would mean the other piled up. Being a solo parent is a tough thing. On top of being the sole income provider as well meant little time for spontaneous fun. However, with time and a house move, I was able to allow that slowly back into our lives. Nevertheless, it takes conscious effort and reminding that spontaneity does, in fact, take practice.

What is spontaneity? It's often something that scares people. Why? Because it approaches the whole routine. People who are spontaneous have a little spark about them; they don't let little moments or opportunities pass them by. I want to explore what spontaneity means for you and how you can learn to practice it daily.

Step one: Funny enough, being spontaneous takes practice.

Step two: Try not to overthink everything and all the "what is".

Step three: Instead of writing to-do lists, make one decision and just do it.

Number 1: How do we become more spontaneous? Funny enough, being spontaneous takes practice.
Some people are naturally spontaneous and grief can put a lid on that. As we become over-thinkers it can take courage and it can be scary. However, if you practice it, trying to bring some spontaneity back into your life, and put in a few practices daily then you'll see it unfold. One way we can do this is by breaking the household routine sometimes. I know, for me, having a routine with young children was really important but often the memories that we hold in our heart from those early years are those of once when we were spontaneous. Like I can remember one time - making a little picnic and just walking across the road to have our dinner at six o'clock at night in a park instead of trying to rush through emotions of dinner about time, and bed. Those are the memories that I know my kids hold in their hearts as well. So, breaking household routines can sometimes be one way of introducing some spontaneity.

Number 2: Try not to overthink everything and all the 'what if's'.
Studies show that overthinking can lead to serious emotional stress. If we don't learn to get out of our head at times, we may be missing out

on so much and struggle to cope with the situations, similar to leading to anxiety disorders. If you're experiencing a number of these symptoms you're more likely dealing with overthinking. It's hard to stay focused in conversations or you're thinking ahead rather than truly listening or you're worried about what people think of you or you are focusing on the negative side rather than the positive outcomes.

Over-planning kills the magic. In 2016, I wanted a trip to Fiji. On a list I carried with me to the trip, I used to program to get healthy and motivated to find strength in fitness again. Winning the challenge was an awesome feeling but straight away my thoughts turned to what if something happened to me while I was away? What if I hurt myself and could no longer work? What if I suffer too many anxiety attacks over there to enjoy myself? Will my kids feel like I'm abandoning them? Will they be okay? Of course, they were in the loving care of their grandparents. If I'd allowed myself to stay in those thoughts for too long, I would have denied myself the trip of a lifetime. I believe all things present to you at just the right time and that time away was exactly what I needed to arrange it then. It brought some adventure and spontaneity back into my life. I returned a much better mummy and in fact, it was a catalyst for me questioning my purpose. We'll cover that in the next chapter. It also gave me vitality and growth, which I think led to meeting my partner at the right time.

So what is overthinking? Simply put - overthinking is to think about something too much for too long. It happens to everyone at some point but coupled with grief, it can be crippling. If I got a dollar every time I caught myself for overthinking, I'd be very rich by now. Overthinking can be catastrophic to living a fun and spontaneous life. I think we tend to overthink as mothers anyway, but if you put that with the fear that comes with the death of a loved one then you have a recipe for paralysis when it comes to acting spontaneously. So, how do we invite that into our life? One way is to let go. It's exhausting to always be focusing on worse case scenarios when thinking about your loved ones or something happening to yourself. Learn to slow down your racing thoughts through breathing and mindfulness. I came back from the fire. Stop and ask yourself, is this true? Has this happened yet? What are the chances of this happening? And be real with your answers. Often you'll find that it will lead you to slow down your thoughts allowing that moment to happen. My mantra, I say to myself out loud is,

> *"Life is too short to miss out on making memories."*

Number 3: Instead of writing a to-do list, make one decision and just do it.
Why this is so effective? Sometimes you can get overwhelmed with lists instead of focusing on one thing and acting on the moments. If we write too big a list, then we get paralysed with thoughts of trying to do all of those things and spontaneity dies. So, often it's better to just write one thing and go with it. When I had returned from my trip to Fiji, I was guilty of having left my kids for a length of time with family. However, the trip had given me a sense of adventure and purpose and I turned that around into the moment of spontaneity. We jumped online to book a night in the city. I called it our city adventure. We all bungled in one room as they were still little enough. We walked everywhere, we went to the museum, the art gallery, ice-skated in King George's square. We ate hot dogs in our apartment and danced on the couches in our pyjamas. I know it was memorable for them because we often talk about it. It was spontaneity that truly created a beautiful memory for us, and it can never be taken away. So what exactly is overthinking? When we get overwhelmed with the 'to-do's' and the 'what if's', it can stop us in our tracks.

I carried this reminder in many situations. Sometimes when a wave of grief washes over you like a tsunami, the best way to replace the pain of loss is to replace your thoughts with happy memories. It, therefore, works the same way when we replace those negative thoughts with some positive action. Just pack a day bag and leave the house. With kids, it's as easy as going to the park or beach. Something will happen to remind you of those small joys again. Another way to introduce this is to; take an unplanned trip, get up and dance at weddings, do something crazy out of routine, or go for a walk after dinner. You might be overthinking about some little actions, but you can take over the day to create spontaneity. Remember, it takes practice to be spontaneous.

We should all learn to smile more often and laugh.
Grief is cruel and heartbreaking, but remember there is so much more room in your heart for more than just pain. Healing is there to be had. Sometimes it is by default that we stack things against us. The sun is going to rise; the sun is going to set.

* * *

> **"LET'S START LIVING AND ENJOY IN BETWEEN."**
>
> **–Xo Rachel**

The meaning of life
  is to find your gift
the purpose of life
  is to give it away
∽ Pablo Picasso ∽

@giftsfromgrief

Chapter 9
The Gift of Purpose

"You are never too old to set a new goal or dream a new dream"
-C.S Lewis

In my mind, in my personal grief story, I picture the baby steps that have led to rediscovering my purpose and the gift of helping others on their grief journey. I'm always looking forward to a bigger purpose because one of the greatest gifts I have been given by the grief is to start living with intent. I certainly wouldn't be here writing this book if I hadn't experienced all the devastating loss in my life. And for me, the heartache and pain I endured, and the growth that came from that, was a necessary part of my story to bring me to where I am today.

My passion is to serve and help others by lifting the lid on conversations around grief, and in turn, help them recognize their own gifts of grief. It is such a healing journey in itself when you learn the gift of a higher purpose for others. I want to help grieving people grow while still learning to heal themselves along the way.

There aren't too many people who haven't questioned their purpose in life. Let me ask you this, "Have you found that loss has caused you to question the meaning of life, and further still, question your true purpose?" It could be that you're feeling lost with no direction, floundering, because a part of you is missing. For me, I realised years later after losing my husband that it was in the "getting lost" that I was reborn and given a new gift of purpose. This is a gift available to us all if we allow the searching, and the sitting in the dark places to happen first. We can't avoid it.

My story, selling my business, living through the shit storm, and discovering my gift of contribution is covered in the next chapter. I want to reassure you also, that when we're talking about purpose and grieving, this chapter is not about trying to overhaul your life overnight. Fact 1: Grief takes grieving. Fact 2: it takes time, and no two timelines are the same. Give yourself some grace, acknowledgement and focus on making one small change at a time. It's then that you'll start to notice the little changes. Baby steps will add up to purposeful transformation. Most of all, don't give up. What I want to do here is to unwrap the gift of purpose and my wish for you is to revisit your own passions. Ask yourself what makes you feel alive, is it helping others? Is it something creative you want to share with the world? Or maybe it's a thirst for knowledge and learning that you haven't yet had the opportunity to study?

Purpose in life is a gift all of us desperately want and need. Grief changes us and gifts us with a new set of eyes, a wider view of life and the world around us. Let's look at some keys to finding your purpose in life while still growing through grief.

Step one: Get out of your head and into your heart, explore your passions.

Step two: Be prepared for the growth, it should challenge you and make you uncomfortable.

Step three: Take action.
So how do we do that?
Let's look at these a little deeper.

Step one: Get out of your head and into your heart.
It is very important to connect to your core and explore your passions allowing yourself to discover what ignites your soul. Taking the time to reflect on your spiritual bliss, whatever that may be, will often lead you to your heart. And it's only with such soul reflection that we can learn to believe for ourselves that we are all born for greatness. When you connect to your true inner self then life is limitless, but first, we need to get out of our thoughts and learn beliefs and patterns. In other words, we need to get out of our own way!

I love this quote from the late Princess Diana: *"Only do what your heart tells you."*

What does it mean to get out of your head and into your heart? I think too often, we get easily distracted by way too much noise and our inner voice or intuition is screaming to be heard. This can be especially true in grief because we can often be clouded with so much fog and heaviness that comes with grieving.

So let's look at how we can get out of our head and into our heart. Often I have to remind myself to not think too much and remember spontaneity whereas humans tend to overthink things, which in turn prevents us from doing what our heart is telling us to do. Trust the process, believe in your heart. Your heart is trying to tell you good things are coming when your head is stuck in the past reminding you of what has happened. Hence, we need to learn to let go of what we can't change - the past, and what we can't predict - the future. We can make daily decisions to live in the present. Therefore, when trying to reconnect spiritually with each moment, take a deep breath and bring yourself back into your heart's space out of your head and later spend time in nature, and breathe deeply, imagine blowing all that chatter into a time and not releasing it into the air. Now your head is clear and ready to receive what your heart is telling you.

Step two: Be prepared for the growth, it should challenge you and make you uncomfortable.
Discovering purpose often requires us to step outside our comfort zone. For us to follow our heart often means doing something against the norm, mostly swimming upstream instead of following the crowd. This can be difficult when dealing with grief too as most of us have some extra facts just to think about before taking a leap of faith. Questioning your purpose while doing so brings so many questions. Is this what I really want? Am I living my full potential? With grief comes a lot of what I mentioned before, brain fog. You need to understand that you don't have to have it all figured out right now. What I'm trying to share though is that by taking time to stop and reflect, it might just be the remedy we need to redirect us on our path to healing. It's truly amazing what happens when you let go what you can't control and take ownership of your own personal growth and challenges. Remember, there's no life without challenges, we all face them. So let's use our gifts of resilience to its full potential.

How you can do that? You can do that by being thankful for your life, by being excited about change and growth. Allow the change to shift. Holding on to your grief and past will eventually suffocate you. It's okay to not be okay, but don't stay there. Every day brings another day for growth and small moments of moving forward. Learn to forgive yourself and others. Build your life around what you love. I love this quote by Socrates "The secret to change is to focus all of your energy not on fighting the old but on building the new."

Step three: Take action.

"In any moment of decision, the best thing you can do is the right thing. The next best thing you can do is the wrong thing. The worst thing you can do is nothing."
-By Theodore Roosevelt

It's not only important to think better for yourself but also to start doing better. I know a good mindset is what we all need and is the best way of making the switch from negative to positive. But sometimes it's just in the doing rather than in the thinking. This is essential for discovering your gift of purpose. Without acting on what your heart is calling us to do, we will spend the rest of their lives wondering and thinking what if I believed. If I had spent just one more month thinking about writing this book and launching my business, I never would have started. Instead of listening to the fear and what was in my head, I started listening to the encouragement from others, "You should definitely write this, Rachel; you will help people."

When I started saying this to myself, I started to act. One conversation at a time. One coffee meeting at a time. And reaching out to all that I've done to what I wanted to do, gathering all the faith I had and just started. So what does it mean to take action? Starting is always the hardest part. And why does that cure fear? I'm here to tell you that the motivation and massive action do not work for grieving. Forget massive action. Let's take action one baby step at a time because when you're grieving, the idea of massive action is just so huge and unachievable that it is bound to stop you right in your tracks.

We tend to forget that the baby steps still move you forward. Remember, having a shower and something to eat is a good day. It's one more positive thing to add to that day. How can we take action? There's so much to be said for just getting up and moving without thinking. Moreover, the simple form of doing can be a huge catalyst for change. And I'm not talking about moving mountains here, we're only capable of what we're capable of right here at this moment, especially in grieving. Nonetheless, for me, I can spend so much time in my head planning, thinking, calculating risk, pros and cons, writing, blah, blah, blah that nothing gets done. If you're scared of failure, and most of us are, then just remember this - there's no falling backwards, it's just falling forward. The more you fall forward, the better you become at whatever task you are trying to achieve. Just keep swimming, meanwhile, if you stop, you'll get swept off in the current of your thoughts, and that will lead to floundering and inaction. You don't have to have it all figured out to move forward, just take the next step.

So if you're stuck wondering what's my purpose when my loved one has gone, now that I don't have my mum or dad cheering me on, now that I don't have the life I'd imagined with my husband or wife or partner, start practicing the art of stepping outside your head, prepare yourself for growth, and take action. Your purpose will unfold gently right before your eyes. What happens next? You see the beautiful gift of contribution when you get to give your purpose away.

A message to a grieving heart:

> **I DON'T HAVE TO TAKE THIS DAY ALL AT ONCE, RATHER, ONE MINUTE, ONE HOUR AT A TIME, ONE BREATH, EVEN ONE BABY STEP, ONE MOMENT AT A TIME. THINGS WILL GET DONE WHEN THEY GET DONE. I AM ONE PERSON, AND I AM MOVING FORWARD, GROWING THROUGH MY GRIEF.**
>
> **–Xo Rachel**

***

there is no
   GREATER AGONY
      than bearing an
         UNTOLD STORY
            inside you
               – m. angelou

@giftsfromgrief

Chapter 10
The Gift of Contribution

"It is not what we get but who we become, what we contribute... that gives meaning to our lives"
–Anthony Robbins

Have you ever had an "on your knees, under the cover of darkness" moment? I can only say I've had a few, crying, screaming, 'where to now', 'I can't do this anymore'.

I just don't know what my future is meant to look like. I pleaded out loud, there has to be some reason as to why I'm still standing. I knew, of course, being a mother to my precious children was one and I'll admit to them being my only reason for getting out of bed on some days. "They truly are a gift, but what about me?" I asked. What am I going to do with all my awareness and growth? I did recognize how far I had come. I did recognize the fact that I was much further down the road in my grief journey, and people were starting to ask me for advice for themselves, or for a friend in need of help. That's when I started thinking, I cannot go through this transformation and not share it with the world. It is only in the awareness of all the gifts I've received, nurtured and developed along the way that have had me come a full circle to the gift of contribution. However, I often imagine if I had stayed stuck under those heavy grief blankets like I had all those years... I shudder to even think about it. Imagine if I had ignored all the signs and all the growth. And one of the contributing factors to learning about all that and discovering my gift of contribution was through some education, and through some reflection, and through

GIFTS FROM GRIEF

learning some things about myself that I may not have noticed before or taken time to rediscover.

One of those is learning about six core needs by Tony Robbins. I'll take that up in this chapter and we'll reference the website here.

Tony Robbins describes the six core needs as certainty and uncertainty, love and significance, and growth and contribution. We have a diagram here depicting those six core needs. Now, let's look at the keys to adding a meaningful contribution to your life.

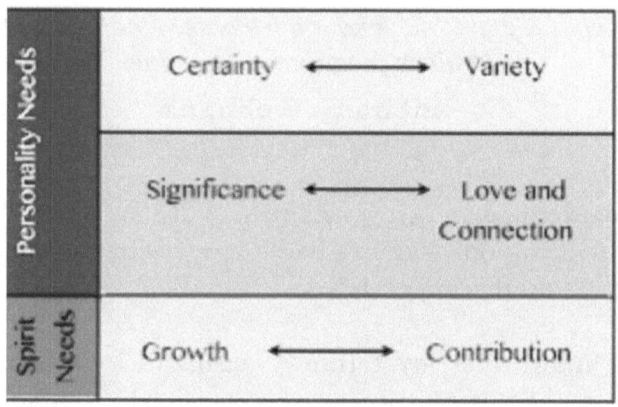

Step one: Familiarize yourself on basic, core needs.

Step two: Focus on your actions and not anyone else's.

Step three: Let's take a seven-day challenge to do one pay-it-forward action per day that you wouldn't normally do.

Step one: Familiarize yourself on six core needs according to Robbins
Each of us should put the six core needs in order of importance. Here, the top four on the list are really the ones that shape our personality and what makes us all different. The last two, growth and contribution, are called spiritual needs. If we take the time to dive into understanding these needs, and which ones you are trying to make, it can help you create new patterns. We all want fulfilment and happiness, and if these needs are not met or are clashing with our behaviours, it can often lead to self-sabotage.

I studied them a while ago to help me with my grief journey and why I was feeling so stuck. Let me share with you a story of my own personal discovery. Of my core needs and co-drivers, two are significance and love and connection. I want to share with you a story about selling my business years after my husband had passed and going back to retail part-time. I thought that I needed to take the time off to be a mum. What I thought and what I wanted, didn't necessarily turn out to be the best for me. I thought it would help me in my healing - To have the time to grieve and to not be so stressed. But what it did lead to was depression and wondering why I wasn't happy. It was as if I was missing significance in my life and why? I had been a manager in the past, and a business owner. It was fulfilling my need to have meaning and pride, and a sense of importance. My previous roles as manager and operator fulfilled that side of me, and my marriage had given me the love and connection that I needed. The result in not filling my need for significance lead to un-resourcefully trying to fill those needs with my kids, by being controlling or over-mothering them, which in turn, wasn't letting them develop **their** sense of significance.

I'm a big-picture person and I need goals and to work towards big dreams. I don't need certainty all the time. Later, when an injury forced me to be home full-time, it was a real lesson for me to realize taking on that role wasn't necessarily going to fulfil me or give me the happiness that I needed to be a good mum.

So what are the six core needs? In brief, let's look at those and then I encourage you to read up and explore them on your own, in your own time. There are plenty of resources explaining them and I really do feel that they go hand in hand with the five languages too. The six human needs as Robbins Research International explains - number one, certainty is the assurance that you can avoid pain and gain pleasure. Number two, uncertainty/variety is the need for the unknown change and new stimuli. Number three, significance means feeling unique, important, special or needed. Number four, connection/love is a strong feeling of closeness or union with someone or something. Number five is growth and expansion of capacity, capability or understanding. And number six, contribution related to a sense of service and focus on helping or supporting others. So how do we know what drives us?

The first four needs, which are certainty, uncertainty, significance and connection, are needs for the self while growth and contribution are needs of the physical body as well as of the spiritual self.

You can only get to the point of growth and contribution once you've met the four physical needs for yourself and that's why it's Important to give yourself something to feel certain about as well as a good blend of something to feel uncertain about. To make sure you're getting significance from somewhere and you have a connection somewhere. That's where you come to a point to be able to grow and contribute. This is, of course, important in all aspects of life, but all the more so when you are dealing with grief. If you want to be able to contribute, you need to make sure that you've given your physical body enough certainty and uncertainty in love and significance.

So how do we know what drives us? We can ask ourselves some questions to reflect upon and discover the core drive in our life at the moment. There are many lessons to this. There are many links online to discover what drives you if you search 'six core needs test' and 'five love languages quiz'

Once you have a clear picture of what drives you, you can start to take small steps daily to fill your own bucket. Remember chapter nine on your purpose and passions. I had to gently remind myself as a widow that it was okay to create new goals for me and let go of old ones. This might be true of old expectations from parents or the ones you may have had with your partner. The ripple effect is that everyone around you will sense your joy and fulfilment. You will, in turn, have **more** time for your loved ones. You'll feel less frustrated and you'll have more love to give. Tony Robbins also has a wonderful Ted Talk on why we do the things we do.

Step two: Focus on your actions, not on anyone else's.
Thinking about others and their actions that may not suit your beliefs or values. It almost always leads to frustrations, appointment, anger or a grudge toward others. This is easier said than done, I know, but don't we just love to hate the quote "The only person you have control over yourself is yourself." All persons change how you see a situation

or remove yourself from it, but you cannot change the other person. Why do we love to hate it is because we know deep down it's true. When I accepted that I couldn't change my situation or how anyone else perceived my personal grief journey, only then I could focus on what I could do at this moment to help me move forward. No one is going to save you, you're in control of your today and your daily decisions tomorrow.

So let's look at how we can focus on our own actions and not others' focus on what you can control. I can't control what happens to my kids each day they leave the house, but I can control my thoughts and actions with mindfulness, breathing and positivity. I choose not to think negatively. Don't focus on your situation but on your trajectory, where you're going to keep your eyes on. The direction is always forward, there's no room for looking back when growing through grief.

Often I say to myself that I can only control my thoughts and my actions/reactions. I tell one thing to myself – what I can change right now would be something that's in my control. How do you react and remember when that grief wave hits you unexpectedly? You do so by saying, "This too shall pass." It won't always be this way, but we can take one day at a time, it's also a reminder that when things are **good** it won't always be this way. So also savour and enjoy every happy moment.

Step three: I want to encourage you to take a seven-day challenge to do one pay forward action per day you wouldn't normally do.
Why is this important? Well, when we take our eyes off our own pain and grieving, it can often be a simple remedy for our own healing. The power of contribution and simple acts of kindness can have extremely positive effects on our moods and our well-being. Some examples are - one smile to a stranger making through a new month, having a cup of tea with someone elderly who might be lonely, or phoning a friend you would normally just text.

There's a lot you can do with the gifts you have been given. Let's put less focus on the problems that aren't up to you to solve, and focus on smaller acts of kindness that are very doable in your circle or community. Remember your list of passions in our 'purpose' chapter. Maybe there's something in there that will not only fill your bucket but by sharing your new passion, you could also help someone else. Take time to journal your good deeds and how they were received, but most importantly, how did it make you feel? A word of caution here, don't overwhelm yourself with everyone's problems or the problems of the world. If we all carried the weight of the world on our shoulders, no one would act or contribute. It would be all too overwhelming.

You can't do it all, but what if we decide to live as if everything we act upon or do, has an effect. Even the little things can have a huge impact and make a difference. Remember, we are not doing these deeds for acknowledgement or anything in return, that's when you know you have powerfully received the gift of contribution. You won't be setting yourself up for disappointment.

* * *

"FEEL THE JOY YOU RECEIVE IN THE GIVING."

–Xo Rachel

- Be still.
- Close your eyes.
- Breathe.
Adventure awaits.

@giftsfromgrief

Chapter 11
The Gift of Adventure

"Why is it only around death that we wake up to life? Don't wait. Live life now."

−Xo Rachel

If you're currently sinking into the deep fold of grief and loss, the last thing on your radar is fun and adventure. Your day-to-day life is more likely fuelled by mere survival and learning to thrive again, rather than diving into a bucket list of adventures. I totally get that. But one of the many subsequent gifts I've learnt to foster, post-loss, is purposely living life again with gusto. We are gifted with the insight to make the memories, to value the moment, and to not let life pass us by. I truly believe that part of our purpose in life is to live the adventure, not just to get by.

I think we stretch ourselves for the better and grow when we take advantage of new adventures. What would life be like if we didn't have a little adventure in it? Adventure brings a more positive and wider view of life; it brings rejuvenation, nurtures your physical being and often brings with it new friendships, excites us, motivates and gives us something to look forward to.

This is quite important when going through the emotions of everyday life while trying to deal with our grief. The catch is, we don't actually feel up for it. Living beyond loss can be exhausting, overwhelming, and very, very grey. It takes courage to step out and realise that it is up to us, or as supporters to re-introduce adventure gently back into our lives.

My late husband Ray loved skydiving and we had this joke (me being a trainee pilot), where I would say, "Why would you jump out of a perfectly good aeroplane?"

The truth is, deep down, I was just petrified with the thought. I do regret never experiencing that with him. One thing he felt so strongly about promoting it was the incredibly euphoric feeling when you're free-falling. What he learnt from his experience was that skydiving plunged a love-life perspective on participants.

I remember Ray expressing that skydiving should be introduced to all mental health programs. Because given the choice when you're free-falling to your potential death, mixed with the rush of adrenaline that it gives you, you receive this experience of, "YES I WANT TO LIVE!" Ray believed that if anyone was experiencing a low and potentially self-harming view on life should give skydiving a go. He was sure that people would always pull the cord at that instant and thus give them a new injection of perspective looking at their life because it just makes you feel so alive.

Now, I'm not saying we should all go out and sign up for skydiving. We must remember that adventure doesn't mean being doubtlessly fearless! It could just mean trying something new, stepping outside our comfort zone or meeting new people, etc.

By inviting a little excitement and adrenaline into your life, you are also inviting a new chance of healing on your grief journey. Who doesn't want that? The world is a big place, but trust me, there's an adventure just outside your front door if you take the time to look for it.

Have you felt that grief and loss have ignited your sense of adventure? Or do you feel you have lost that sense altogether, through fear of circumstance and a lack of lustre for life? If it is the latter, I invite you to explore what excites you through pictures, scrapbooking, YouTube, videos, and dream boards. Take the time out to create a small list of adventure items just for you. What makes your heart sing? Is it gardening, bushwalking, mountain climbing, cycling, art, swimming?

Adventure is something that provides us with a breath of fresh air from our everyday lives. So let's dive deep and look at **seven reasons to embrace a little adventure,** and why it's Important in healing your grief.

1. It gives you the opportunity to try something new.
2. It invigorates the mind and stops you from dwelling.
3. It delivers a renewed sense of accomplishment.
4. Often adventure will reconnect you with the power of being in nature.
5. It gives you the courage to step outside your comfort zone.
6. This, in turn, nurtures growth.
7. It teaches you to face uncertainty head-on. This builds resilience in us all for future endeavours and challenges that may come our way.

Who knows the butterflies in the stomach from feeling scared or unsure about something? It naturally tests us. The truth is, you'll only grow if you're willing to sit through the scared and uncomfortable situations of trying something new. For most of us, it is easier to stay safe and secure in our own current circumstances. I certainly have been guilty of staying under my grief blanket because even though extremely painful, it was easier than stepping out from beneath it. That would mean exposure and vulnerability as we talked about earlier. But it is here where the growth and empowerment happen.

One of my greatest memories is travelling overseas to Europe with Ray shortly after my brother had passed away. Ray had travelled extensively before, but I had only visited New Zealand with my parents when I was 16. So the thought of being in many foreign non-English speaking countries terrified and excited me all at the same time. I could have stayed in my fear of something happening to me, or worried about my Mum and family while I was away. I'm so glad I didn't allow that to deter me from the adventure that awaited us! It was in the early 2000s and so much has changed in the world since then. It was really a magical carefree trip with very few set plans.

We visited Ray's relatives in Ireland, but the rest, we mostly hopped from trains and buses with no real agenda. What an adventure! For over six weeks, we backpacked all around England, Ireland, France and Italy. I was totally scared having never travelled overseas, and definitely being with someone who was an experienced traveller made it a little bit easier. There are so many guided, safe tours, retreats and adventure trips available these days. It is totally doable on your own if considering an adventure abroad. It was one of the best memories that I have ever created, and if I hadn't been willing to step outside my comfort zone and trust in the whole process, I probably would have never taken that trip.

I believe it was the new perspective on life that was gifted to me after my brother had passed away, that allowed me to grow. I knew that he would have loved the thought of me going on this adventure, and I thought about my brother the whole time.

So let's look at the first step - It is to embrace a little adventure into your life. Remember, this is one of the many steps we can take to move forward in our grief. Firstly, we must be open to trying something new and setting some intentions. These five tips will help you get started.

Number one: Step Outside
Like I mentioned earlier, an adventure doesn't have to necessarily mean skydiving or climbing Mt. Everest, it can be as simple as exploring your own neighbourhood parks and gardens or being a tourist in your own town. Anything that helps you to be present and notice the beauty that surrounds us every day. When we step outside, other than our work to home or daily errands, we're getting back to nature, and that helps heal your soul. Not to mention the many health benefits as well. It is well known that getting outdoors reduces stress, anger, fear, and increases endorphins creating more pleasant feelings. It is a go-to for me when I get a wave of grief or anxiety to overcome me. The ocean is one of my many happy places. I feel instantly at ease when I can see, smell, and experience the beauty of the ocean. For you, it may be a beautiful garden, the fresh mountain air, or the bush. Find what makes your soul speak to you and seek that. In this technological age, it is more important than ever to take the time to step away from our devices and soak in some fresh air.

Number two: Hang around adventurous "positive life" seeking people
Who you hang out with, rubs off. It is a sure recipe for developing healthy self-esteem, adventurous spirit, and more compassionate

personality when you learn to attract adventurous, fun-loving people into your life. Secondly, it is a positive way to move forward in your grief. I find it is in the honour of those I've loved and lost to be around people who admire and are like them. There are plenty of meet-up groups that have a variety of activities for all levels, from bushwalking to salsa dancing.

Step out and join a group, it may be daunting in the first visit, but trust me, you won't look back once the fun and laughter start. Let their love of life and energy rub off on you. You may not feel ready to do this on your own, so talk to a friend who can come with you. Remember baby steps, but just meeting people who aren't in your family circle can give you a break from living with your grief 24x7. Or alternatively, it can give you the opportunity to talk about your loss in a different environment. One thing I quickly discovered was that by mentioning my circumstances, sure enough, there was always someone in the group who understood and was experiencing a similar grief journey to mine. This can be such a relief when the people close to you no longer know what to say or how to help. God has a wonderful way of allowing people into your life when you need them the most. It is truly one of the most awe-inspiring gifts from my grief… the people I would never have met if it wasn't for my loss. Sharing adventures with others make them even more enjoyable.

Number three: Learning to say 'yes' when our grief is trying to hold us back
We've all said 'no' to a fun event or adventure that we may have regretted later. This is perfectly normal in the depths of our grief because of our automatic flight or fright reaction. We may need to feel safe, or not want to get hurt or feel like we don't have the energy to do something out of our ordinary routine. Often people will try to help in your grief journey by asking you to do things or go to events, and it's really easy to just say no straight away because that's comfortable. But I'm here to tell you, it's the shakeup in your routine that gives you a burst of energy and the desire to do something else a little more adventurous.

Business or local social networking events can be a fun way to meet people and learn new things along the way. Everyone has a story and something to share. You can come away feeling quite uplifted by attending events that have inspiring speakers share their stories. The first time might feel daunting, but I go to them all the time on my own now and always end up meeting some great people.

Number four: Be creative
It might mean taking up the craft you've dreamt of doing or attending an art class. Journaling or scrapbooking, when you feel strong enough to go through photos, is another creative outlet to move through your grief in a healthy way. Use your strong moments, your future self will thank you. All of these small acts spark adventure in the spirit. I know going through photos can plunge you into a deep ocean of tears, but this is also healthy. Crying is necessary. Outrageous punching into a pillow is healthy. Don't avoid the act because of fear of breaking down. What you might find id something beautiful and creative will come out of it, like a tribute frame, or collage that will provide healing for your future.

I also want to touch on de-cluttering, in the topic of being creative, because when you are dealing with your loved one's belongings, that's being adventurous in itself. Working out what to keep and what to give away can be very daunting, but if viewed as a creative venture, it can be more liberating than making you sad. My Mother hand-painted and made a beautiful planter out of one of Ray's work boots. Letting go of the things that have held memories or personal items of your loved ones can be a very hard task. And it took several years of looking at things with new eyes every year, deciding whether to hold on to certain things or not. Once I realised that a lot of treasures were my husband's and not mine, it became easier to keep the special things that held a place in my heart. After all, I don't expect my children to lug around my childhood netball trophies, do I? For me, I discovered that a lot of things that were important to Ray from his childhood he would hold on to because they were important to him not necessarily to me. So, in the end, I created a few large storage boxes for our kids filled with special memory books, trinkets and photos, his watch and cufflinks, and things that were significant to their early childhood with their Daddy. When we moved house, it was really liberating to downsize them to a few boxes that I can give to the kids later. So my advice to you is to be adventurous and creative in your de-cluttering. Ask for help if you need.

Number five: Take occasional sabbaticals from social media.
I read a great picture quote that said: *"Let's wander where the Wi-Fi is weak."*

Going offline can be a great way to reconnect with what YOU love, not what everybody else is doing and loves. Suddenly widowed at 38, with two young children early to bed, I admit to a period of my life post-loss, where I was depressed with "compassion syndrome". This was purely because of my time on social media, mindlessly scrolling at what I perceived as everybody else's "perfect" family life. Mine was taken from me, and I became increasingly angry, bitter and depressed by what I filled my mind with every night. Friends, strangers, celebrities… you name it, I was COMPARING. This is not healthy for anyone, and increasing studies are showing the significant effect this (social media) has on our mental health.

I was allowing myself to be swept up into everybody else's perceived perfect world, especially at an age where everyone had young children out and about, playing happy families and I was, at that time, home alone STARING AT THE FOUR WALLS WONDERING HOW THE HELL DID I GET HERE? Lucky for me, I recognised the dangers and quickly learnt to separate myself from this world on a number of sabbaticals. What I noticed was that when I was offline, I started creating my own family adventures. Just the three of us…bike-riding, climbing mountains, eating out, weekends away. It was still lonely at times, but I felt so liberated knowing that I was capable. Proud also, that I was the creator of memories for my kids.

I think we've all stopped living in the present, at times. Being in the moment, away from our phones, allows us to start taking care of ourselves and others around us. The purpose of inviting some adventure into your life is to help you grow through your grief in a more healthy and healing way. These are all small building blocks to a happier you, post-loss.

One of the most significant turning points for me, to allowing more adventure into my life, was going to Fiji on an adventure retreat,

3 years after my husband's passing away. Firstly, I must add, I won the trip out of dedication to my fitness and health journey committing fully to Lisa Curry's 12-week KISS program. Knowing that I had achieved something for myself post-loss, in view of my young children's eyes, was an incredible gift on its own. But to win such an amazing trip as well, was going to be one of the biggest adventures of my life. I knew nobody, but after one incredible week, I made friends for life #fijifungirls.

You deserve the investment in yourself, to join a gym or club, to book a holiday or retreat. Believe me, the alternative might lead to costing you more in ill-health and general well-being down the track, than the investment to save for such a self-loving gift. By living by example for my kids, not being afraid to try new things, or meet new people, I allowed the fog to lift. I have never looked back when it comes to dreaming of my next big adventure.

* * *

> **ADVENTURE FILLS YOUR SOUL. IT'S THE ONE WAY TO MAKE THE MOST OUT OF LIFE, AS IT ALLOWS YOU TO LOOK UPON LIFE ITSELF AS AN ADVENTURE.**
>
> –Xo Rachel

Today I...
→ Am at peace with the past
→ Have gratitude for the present
→ And look forward to what's next

@giftsfromgrief

Chapter 12
Gift of Empowerment
(Wholehearted Living)

"It takes courage to grow up and become who you really are"
-E.E.Cummings

I never imagined I would be 44 years old before arriving at a space of empowerment and wholehearted living. But I guess, if we allow the lessons and awareness into our hearts, we will always be learning and growing. When you find yourself at a spot where none of it was in your life plan, years of getting knocked down, and getting back up again, I discovered I had many life questions that led me to rediscover my soul's purpose. To find joy in all that is life, the messy and the magic, is when it all comes together. We can't avoid the pain or the setbacks, so there has to be some sense in surrender. To embrace our grief as well as our growth, and take notice of everything in between. I truly do believe this is where we lose ourselves along the way, and miss making the memories. When we lose sight of what is really important.

My Gift of Empowerment (wholehearted living) is a result of me fully recognising and receiving all of the gifts outlined in chapters one to eleven. My gift of empowerment is to teach this to others so that they don't have to take that long on their grief journey to start living a full life again. I know, for me, there were too many years where I wrapped myself up in my grief blanket, which prevented me from living my best life.

I want you as a reader to take a hold of your very own personal gift box and start to unravel what is inside all of these gifts bundled into one beautiful box, waiting for you to unwrap for yourself. If you are willing to lift the lid, there lies the gift of living a wholehearted, joyful life, while still allowing yourself to grieve in a way that allows self-care and healing.

I want to ask you, "What does your wholehearted day look like?" Would it be fair to say that I know it **doesn't** involve non-stop tears, pain and heartbreak? That it is **NOT** living stuck, and on repeat. That I know it **doesn't** look like anger, denial, and blame and that it is not dull and tainted with fear.

Believe me, I have lived plenty of those days and I want you to know that you are not alone. I know in my heart, your wholehearted day holds memories that make you smile, adventures that create new ones, and daily decisions that make you proud.

> A person working towards self-empowerment is able to take control of their life and start making positive daily decisions for moving forward.
> Remember, you are still allowing yourself to grow through your grief. This is something I'm so passionate about, in educating people that it is a necessary emotion. We are not sweeping it under the carpet and pretending life is wonderful 24x7! My wish for you is to gently crash through the barriers of grief one day at a time, embrace the gifts, allowing them to become your superpowers!

So what do you mean by "empowerment"?
The dictionary says it is the process of becoming stronger and more confident, especially in controlling one's life and claiming one's rights.

I truly believe empowerment is the gift to help oneself, and here's the bonus gift:

Once you have the gift of empowerment, i.e. the ability to help yourself grow through grief, you then have the power to gift someone else the opportunity to help themselves, in leading by example.

Let's look at some keys to working toward personal empowerment on your grief journey:

1. Take time out to reflect and reinvent
2. Develop daily habits with simple daily decisions
3. Focus on what is in YOUR control

Step 1. Take time out to reflect and reinvent
In life, we often don't take the time to stop and reflect on how far we've come.

Sometimes I feel like I've lived three lives – my childhood, my life before kids/ pilot days, and my life now. And I often ignore those achievements because it also brings up a time of loss for me. Taking the time out to reflect and reinvent means that we get to really stop and reflect on what is serving us now and what we can let go of. Also, hanging on to old values or truths we tell ourselves when we have grown so much, can often be the very thing that is holding us back. Sometimes we need to clear out the cobwebs, boring light to the positive achievements in our lives and focus on how the lessons learnt from that can bring new successes to our current life.

Let's look at how we can bring awareness to that:
Write three things down you could eliminate from your life, which you truly believe in your heart are not serving you to create a wholehearted life.

Now write three things you think you have been wanting to add into your life, which you know deep down will gift you that sense of empowerment and control.

1————————————   1————————————
2————————————   2————————————
3————————————   3————————————

By reflecting and caring deeply for yourself and those around you, you are embracing the gift of growth and awareness for where you are right now in this moment. Knowing who you are, acknowledging what you have been through and what you now have to offer others is a wondrous gift.

What's next?
With this awareness comes the rebirth or reinvention of the new you. Someone who has seen death and loss, but also someone who has the ability to reflect on life from a different perspective. Someone who has the gift of gratitude and growth leading them to a better life.

Step 2. Develop daily habits with daily decisions
What daily decisions are we making now that are just habits from our past?

And what new ones can we create that will serve us better to move forward through our grief? By creating a new normal with these small daily decisions we then create new habits, in mind and body, which in turn is the greatest way to grow through your grief. I know, for me, one of the biggest discoveries on my healing journey was to revisit my own personal health and physical well-being. When you are a caregiver for someone full-time, it can really take a toll on your own health and well-being. By making a decision to move my body daily post-loss was the catalyst for many other new normal things in my life. Plus the added benefit of setting an example to my kids for ways to positively do things for yourself.

A habit is a routine or a ritual that is repeated regularly and tends to occur subconsciously or automatically.

Over a period of time, these create an effect, good or bad, on our minds and bodies.

How can we develop daily habits with conscious daily decisions for a better way to receive the gifts outlined in our first chapters?

Each morning, we get up and go through our daily rituals. Several, even before leaving the house.

Each morning, we can choose a healthy breakfast or we can skip it. We can choose to play uplifting music or we can put on the news channel (mostly bad news). We can choose to rush out the door or we can take **a minute** to be fully present in the arms of our loved ones. We can tell them we love them and that we wish for them to have a great day, or we can ignore them. Choices! Later in the day, we can choose to get angry over spilt milk or road rage, or we can choose to say, "Oh, well! That's that, and this too shall pass."

These are what I call daily decisions. The same goes for the evenings... you get my drift. The reason I chunk it down is that we can get overwhelmed with all that needs to be done in a week, month, year, but the reality is – healthy healing and growth come from the stacking of simple, good daily decisions over time.

"You'll never change your life until you change something you do daily. The secret of your success is found in your daily routine"
–John C. Maxwell

Daily
We can practice our daily ritual of gratitude
We can write down and recognise how far we've come on our grief journey
We can deliver simple acts of kindness to others
We can push ourselves outside our comfort zone and do something adventurous
We can be spontaneous and nurture one of our core needs for a variety

We will expand on these in our bonus chapter!

Step 3 Focus on what is in your control
This is a tough one, mentally. Accept reality, bad things are going to happen.

People will hurt you, people die, and it's the circle of life. I'm not saying by accepting these realities, we will take the pain away, but at least we will not set ourselves up for total devastation. Acceptance brings you to reality, and with that, you have a starting point to healing your pain. It allows us to be more present in the now because we have accepted what will happen in the future. It's just that none of us knows when this time is, so the purpose is to accept but not live in fear or sadness for the future. When you remember the good things and the gifts you have gained, you are less likely to remain stuck in your grief.

What it means is to focus on what is in your control, to know that you will always face plenty of loss and heartache, everyone does, and it's a part of life. You cannot control when it is someone's time. The real reality is:

How you attack each day **IS** in your control i.e. your attitude.

Remember our gratitude gift. Also, practice the art of forgiveness, life's too short to hold on to past wrongs. None of us is perfect. Let's not let our own egos get in the way of a family being united.

It goes without saying then, that if we stay focused on our loss, then it is one sure way of stripping you of gratitude. Learn to let go of past wounds. They are not there to serve your future. You are in control of your daily decisions.

What's next?

Your life was not meant to be lived in a state of just survival.
Your life is meant to be LIVED.
If you are young and reading this, you have been given the gift of perspective early. You know how precious life is and how not to take each day for granted.
Now that we know there is a gift of empowerment from grief, we can move forward with a sense of responsibility and ownership, and my hope is that we will not let our grief own us. But WE can own our grief.

There is a catch…
Reading this book, or doing a course, joining a group or gym, is not going to fix you. If you are in a place where you are feeling stuck in your grief, with no drive to get out there and live the adventure that life is, there is only one person who can change that for the better. I know it's hard. I know it hurts. But it is not forever. It does get better. If you allow it.

In my bonus chapter, we will take a snapshot of all these Gifts from Grief.

We will lift the lid on your grief box and outline practical ways to empower you to take responsibility for your own happiness and life.

> I am ALIVE and I have survived
> I am still here for a reason

Living a wholehearted life is the best way I can honour my loved ones

* * *

"NEVER BEND YOUR HEAD. ALWAYS HOLD IT HIGH. LOOK THE WORLD STRAIGHT IN THE EYE."

–Helen Keller

Wishing you
STRENGTH for today
&
HOPE for tomorrow

@giftsfromgrief

Chapter 13
Bonus Chapter
Let's Lift the Lid

"We rise by lifting others"
-Robert Ingersoll

How do we help grieving friends and family?
A. How do we help grieving friends and family?
B. What is coming up for you? - A space to heal

How do we help grieving friends and family?
There were days when I was overwhelmed with support and help from family and friends AND there were days where I felt completely alone. This is a part of grief we all have to learn. As a grieving Mum, there came a day when I had to cope on my own and stand on my own two feet. It was hard, exhausting and painful, but the strength that came from doing that was worth the climb.

"You don't know how strong you are until being strong is your only choice"
-Bob Marley

In the first part of this bonus chapter, I want to cover some really helpful tips for those wanting to help someone in their time of need. It is not something we are taught and I'm sure many of you can relate to not knowing what to say or do. You may be afraid of intruding, saying the wrong thing, or simply not knowing how you can help.

"Let me know if there is anything I can do?" Does this sound familiar?

Well, I'm here to share that as a grieving person, we will NOT reply with a list of things we need help with or doing. This is very common because, for one, you can't think straight in the early days/months of grief, and number two, it is often hard to accept help if you are naturally independent or going through a very private journey especially with illness.

Below is a list of 12 things you can do and several ways to bring up conversations down the track to check in on your friend or family member. Your comfort and support can make a huge difference to someone's healing. While you can't take away the pain, there are many ways to show someone how much you care.

Practically:
1. Try not to avoid your friend or family member who has just been through a heartbreaking loss. This can add to their heartbreak when they feel like nobody cares. If you can't visit in person, a call, text, or email is still comforting to let them know that you are thinking of them. Be honest, if you don't know what to say or do, tell them. "I'm sorry, I don't know what to say, I know I can't take away the pain but I want to help in some way if I can."
At least they know you are there, and that can open up the next acts of kindness listed below, by you just showing up. They will let you know if they feel overwhelmed with family or visitors at the moment, which allows you time to check in at a later date.

2. Just show up
    1. Do something you are naturally good at e.g. if cooking is something you love to do then just let them know you would like to drop some food off for them and if they are not home, you will leave in a cooler box at the door. That way, if they don't feel like talking just yet, they still can receive your kindness in a way that would be very helpful.
    2. Boxes of essentials are also very helpful in the early stages of grief. Think - toilet paper, tissues, wash liquid, nappies if they have small children, large tins of coffee, drinking chocolate,

spreads, biscuits, and pantry items, or even an online grocery voucher for them to get home delivery.

3. If patience and paperwork are your specialties, then offer to come around and tick off some pressing tasks that may seem upsetting or overwhelming. Just the act of sitting on hold for them to phone companies, insurance, etc. so that they can jump on when ready to talk is a huge help. Also, accompanying them to offices and government agencies can be very supportive. I can remember really breaking down in a heap, after a visit to one of these, to fill out widow and parenting paperwork, and I felt so alone.
4. Offer help with babysitting or take them out on a short outing to soothe their soul with some nature or comforting tea. Remember, it's the little things that are so very hard, so saying you will come and pick them up might just prompt them to do something away from their house that can be very healing. They may not want to be surrounded by a lot of hustle and other families so choose your outing wisely, somewhere quiet where you can just sit with them or help watch their kids play in a park with a takeaway coffee.
5. Mow their lawn, clean their house, widows, laundry service (or organise a collection from friends to pay some people who can). The value in this is self-explanatory and worth the world when exhausted from grieving.
6. Contact people for them, if they need help with getting through notifying more people outside their family and friends' circle.
7. Offer to help with going through some personal items of their loved one, to put away. This is a very personal and heartbreaking task that needs compassion and understanding. There are many things that they might want to hold on to, that you don't necessarily see the sentiment in. Do not judge. Be kind and helpful to place those in storage boxes to be revisited at a later stage. It is very important to not make rash decisions as a grieving person OR have them made for you when not thinking clearly. If there are children involved, it is important to think ahead of what they may value when they are older. I have done up two storage boxes for Amelia and Vincent to look through when they are bigger and they can then decide on what they might want to keep (of their Dad's).

Emotionally:

8. Do not try and fix them or stop them from crying. Even the best intention can seem as though you are shutting them out. Just be present even if in silence. Allowing them to grieve openly is very healthy and stress relieving. A gentle touch or hug to know you are there is enough. Remember also, if the person is not crying, that's okay too, everyone deals with their emotions differently. It's your presence that counts.
9. Share stories and happy memories of their loved one. They want to hear their name and feel moments of laughter and joy in memories. Bring photos or items that they may love to see. This will help soothe them even if it still makes the tears flow.
10. Understanding the grieving process will better equip you to help a bereaved friend or family member. (Hopefully, I've provided some insight in the first twelve chapters)

    Know that there is no right or wrong way to grieve and that it can be an emotional rollercoaster for many years to come. Do not put time frames on their grief, or suggest where they should be at a certain time after. A grieving person may lash out, act out of character, or be emotionally unstable, depressed and angry. Try not to take any of this personally in such a situation, it just means they feel safe in allowing their emotions to flow around you. Understand that they will not always feel this way, and you being there will help with that growth and healing.

11. Knowing what to say is often better rephrased as knowing when to just listen.

    Acknowledgement is the number one way to show that you recognise their pain but may not know the right thing to say. Letting them know you are there to listen can often be enough. That way, if done with compassion, you can read more cues from the grieving person as to how the conversation may go or how you can help. Avoiding or changing the subject can often make your friend feel isolated and that their loved one is forgotten.

    Some simple things you can say, which can let them see that the death of their loved one is acknowledged and your concern is expressed, are:

"I heard your ____ died, I'm so sorry this has happened to you. I'm here for you."

"Do you feel like talking?" Or "I don't know what to say. This is devastating news, and I want you to know that I care."

The acknowledgement is the most important part, allow your grieving friend to lead. They may open up and share a story or let you know how they are feeling. Having someone listen is the best thing people can offer at times.

12. Things to avoid saying:
    This is touchy, but I have learnt a lot through sharing my journey with others in my Gift from Grief community, and there is certainly a common thread when it comes to saying awkward things in times of loss. I won't comment on them all, but know that they may or may not have the same beliefs as you and it is not your place to say, keep your beliefs to yourself.

    "He is in a better place now"

    "It is part of God's / The Universe's plan"

    "It wasn't meant to be" – this is especially important for infant and pregnancy loss

    "Look at the good side...at least He died instantly and didn't suffer" (accident)

    OR "at least you got to say goodbye and have more time" (illness)

    "You have your whole life ahead of you...and so much to be thankful for" – at such a time, this is not what a grieving person's focus is on. They know there are worse situations, but right now that is not important to them.

    "You should, or you will..." any statements that tell a grieving person what they should or shouldn't be feeling are not helpful or comforting in any way.

Most of all, do not compare one situation to another, or your grief experiences to someone else's. Everyone's journey is different and the only way for them to grieve is to grieve howsoever they can, in their own time.

Encouragement is for gently acknowledging that you admire their strength and grace in a situation they did not choose to be in.

B. What is coming up for you?
Something magical happened on an overcast and windy day. The date was September 11, 2015; Ray's birthday, three years after his passing away. We wandered down the path to the beach that led to our special place. My babes and I were celebrating the birth-date of our wonderful Man.

Vincent picked up a stick and wrote in the sand
  "Happy B'day Daddy"

We took some flowers in a basket and waded out in the shallows of the wild open beach. Each of us throwing splashes of red, blue and pink into the air.

It was in that moment I felt a pull, a deeper meaning to my pain. I looked at Amelia and Vincent going through the motions of a tradition I had created, in the loving memory of their Daddy. One we would continue to do year after year, and still do, to this day. This was Ray's choice of a peaceful resting place, before making his way home. Deep in the sea with a view of the mountains, he loved to ride his mountain bike. The place we flew over, on a joy flight, just weeks before he passed. I love this place. It no longer makes me sad. The ocean is the place I go to in my mind, deep diving under the waves when I feel overwhelmed with grief. I just close my eyes and take myself to the thousands of sweet memories woven into good times. It was my freedom in childhood, my teenage escape, and our family memories all in one. The ocean was where our lives were carefree.

A flicker of hope was ignited in my heart that day, and it was at that moment I made the decision that I would celebrate my love's life as well as celebrate my own. That I would mourn the loss in all its tragedy and heartbroken mess, but I would also choose to live. Not just for my children but for ME, and for my children's children. This would be the ultimate act of respect to Him, my Dad and my Brother. To be a trailblazer in life after loss. To BE an example of happiness after pain. To choose that my circumstances do not define me, but to allow them to shape me.

So now it's your turn…

What's coming up for you and how can you gently show yourself some compassion, some healing and some light on the new journey of your Life? How can you recognise your gifts, and what do they have in store for you for the wonderful life ahead of you?

The following pages hold space just for you. My wish is that by taking some reflective time for yourself, a little flicker of hope will ignite in *your* soul. One that will continue to fuel the fire for you to live.

We are going to recap my twelve discovered gifts and use some exercises to unwrap some takeaways for you.

1. GRATITUDE:

Introducing daily gratitude exercises into your routine has known benefits to overall wellbeing and mood. This is especially helpful when dealing with grief and learning to pull ourselves out of a rut.

Let's look at some practical ways to do this. I wanted to leave space for you to jot some thoughts down. Consider things, people, events, places, and activities. If it feels right, continue to do so in a notebook, journal, voice record or type out on your computer. Whatever works for you, remember to let the thoughts flow freely without self-judgement. This is purely for you.

1. Record 3 things you are grateful for:

_____

_____

_____

_____

Take one of these and write WHY you are grateful. This helps emote the feelings attached.

WHY? _____

2. Write down something GOOD that has happened this week:

_____

_____

_____

_____

3. Finish this sentence, I am GRATEFUL for who I am because…

_____

_____

_____

_____

4. Volunteer: Write down 3 organisations, networks, or groups in your community that you think you would align with if you were to give 1 hour a week/month etc. Put in your diary to contact them this week.

_____

_____

_____

_____

Further activities:

* Take a gratitude walk - no phone, just you, nature and your surroundings. Choose your happy place, the beach, bush, mountains, or wherever fills your soul with a sense of wellbeing.
* Write thank-you letter/card to someone you appreciate. Tell them why their friendship, support means so much to you.
* Do something to treat yourself, a massage, treatment, concert, activity.

Reflect upon your present blessings, of which every Man has plenty; not on your past misfortunes, of which all Men have some."
-Charles Dickens

"THANK YOU" is the best prayer that anyone could say. I say that one a lot. Thank you expresses extreme gratitude, humility, understanding.
-Alice Walker

The real gift of gratitude is that the more grateful you are, the more present you become.
-Robert Holden

Happiness cannot be travelled to, owned, earned, worn or consumed. Happiness is the spiritual experience of living every minute with love, grace, and gratitude.
-Denis Waitley

2. GROWTH:

What I have learnt from sharing my journey with more and more people from all over the world is that although the world is full of suffering and heartbreaking loss, it is also full of overcoming it. I can draw on my own growth as well as learning from those around me who have survived and come out stronger for the pain.

When you begin to recognise yourself for the incredible human being that you are, you will raise your self-esteem and self-care practices naturally. This, in turn, helps us to keep moving forward, making positive steps along the way on our personal grief journey.

Let's lift the lid on some of your own growth:

1. List 5 achievements you are proud of

_____

_____

_____

_____

2. Interrupt un-resourceful habits with new ones. Personal growth happens when we let go of what no longer serves us. If we create a new normal with some positive actions, we can change our lives for the better.

List 3 things that no longer serve you on a daily basis and 3 things you can introduce immediately into your daily routine.

E.g. skipping breakfast - healthy smoothie, or sitting down to food at the end of the day - to 10 mins meditation or stretching

Let go of:	Introduce:
_____	_____
_____	_____
_____	_____

3. Growing through Grief: Find ways to recognise the positive changes you have made walking along your grief road. Revisit some ideas that might help with some unfinished emotions or avoidance when allowing yourself to grieve healthily. Although this might bring up some painful emotions, remember that the only way through grief is to grieve.

Here are some ideas. You might like to jot down which raise some awareness for you.

* "Talk" with your loved one you have lost. Say whatever is on your mind, even things you have wished you said when they were alive.

* Practice Forgiveness. For yourself, regrets, past wrongdoings, and for those who have passed. Accepting that all relationships experience difficult times, and it is important to give yourself, and your loved one, the gift of forgiveness. Write a kind letter to yourself or someone you are wanting to forgive.

* Revisit some personal belongings and see which ones you truly treasure, and which ones you might be ready to let go of. Remember, some items were special to your loved one from THEIR childhood and not a memory for you. This will help you feel lighter and refreshed.

* Honour your loved one by remembering their best qualities and bringing them into your life. What can you be more of? E.g. adventurous, compassionate, loyal

_____

_____

_____

* Reach out to others for help in areas you may feel stuck. E.g. unfinished business, documents, house chores. People are waiting for you to ask them and do not know what it is you need.

List 3 things that are urgent and pressing on your mind daily and a name who you think might help in this area.

Item/chore	Name/support contact
_____	_____
_____	_____
_____	_____

* Take some time to re-prioritise what is important to YOU. Some goals or ideas that keep presenting themselves to you in your mind. More of this below in adventure and purpose.

GUTS & GRACE
It takes courage to try new things. It takes guts to step outside your comfort zone to meet new people. It certainly takes grace to walk your grief journey alone, and even more so to start talking openly about it to help others while helping yourself. What takes the most guts though, is to face your own grief head-on. No one is going to save you and together we must learn how to help others save themselves.

There are many ways I've learnt to reignite the spark and desire for living a more fulfilled life beyond lost. Hopefully, the chapters have given you some new perspective on your own Grief journey and lit a tiny spark within you.

Below is some space for you to write what comes up for your reflection on my box of

Gifts from Grief. Let's unwrap some for you, and you can expand on these in your own journal.

3. PERSPECTIVE:

List some new outlooks on the life you now have because of what you've been through. How can I see myself in this new light? How is my situation gifting me a new perspective because of my growth? E.g. I now appreciate the little things I took for granted before...

_____

_____

_____

_____

4. COMPASSION:

What are some of the qualities you have gained because of your story? You are what you have grown through, not what happened to you.

E.g. I am now more patient and understanding of others, or I give more because I know what it is like to receive. Remember, compassion also includes self-compassion.

_____

_____

_____

_____

5. RESILIENCE:
List some of your achievements that you would never have done if it hadn't been for your loss. E.g. move house, travel, change jobs. Take the time to recognise how far you've come.

_____

_____

_____

_____

6. VULNERABILITY:

Watch Brene Brown's TED talk on Vulnerability
Some exercises I found hard at first, but the more I opened up, the more I learnt about other people's stories as well.

1. Practice answering honestly to yourself and others when asked, "How are you?"
   E.g. instead of answering, "I'm fine", try "I'm okay, but I've been struggling with _____ this week."

2. Speak openly about your challenges, and ask for help.

3. Challenge people's comments if they are upsetting you, maybe with a gentle reminder, "I know you are trying to understand, but saying that upsets me."

4. Be honest with yourself: Becoming aware of our own weaknesses and areas we need to address in our own lives can be the starting point to growth and healing.

7. LOVE (AMPLIFIED):

Understanding that everyone's grief journey is unique, helps us recognise that the loss of a loved one takes time. Life must go on, and learning to honour the love that was lost, while still allowing yourself the ability to experience love again is something only you can grow through. I speak from a Widow's perspective but also relate to the void that losing a parent or sibling, causes us to put up a wall for allowing affection into our lives because of further fear of loss.

Write down some of the 'amplified feelings' loss has gifted you, some we may see as negative. E.g. more fearful, more passionate, more sensitive, more giving. By writing them down, at least we bring awareness to how we are feeling, and also the recognition that it's okay to feel this way.

_____

_____

_____

_____

8. SPONTANEITY:

Introducing some spark and spontaneity into your life is a sure fire to remind you of what you used to enjoy in life before the loss. It is important to let go of expectations on yourself and it does take practice, but you can prepare yourself for some fun activities that will bring some laughter and joy back into your life.

Write down some ideas that would be totally out of the routine in your weekly schedule. Then, put some post-it reminders on your mirror, car or fridge to remind you to grab your bag and head out the door. E.g. Dinner outdoors, see a sunrise, go to the movies on your own, take a road trip to visit a friend.

_____

_____

_____

_____

9. PURPOSE:

Remind yourself of some of YOUR core values. Take the time to write down the things that are of utmost importance to you in moving forward post-loss. E.g. health, family, career path, service to others. Then start researching/reading/talking to people who have success and abundance in these areas. Like-minded people will cross your path once you open yourself up to all possibilities.

My Core Values:

_____

_____

_____

_____

10. CONTRIBUTION:

There are many benefits to volunteering and contributing to those less fortunate than ourselves. I know, for me, volunteering helped to counteract the effects of stress, anxiety and depression around my own future post-loss. It genuinely makes you happy.

Write down some organisations or service groups which you think might suit your talents and personality and how much time you think is realistic for your lifestyle and workload.

E.g. if you love cooking, then a soup kitchen might be perfect, or if you have hidden music talents then playing for local nursing homes is always welcomed.

I could give _____ hours per month

Organisations to contact:

_____

_____

_____

_____

11. ADVENTURE:
Your own personal bucket list ... to do, see, or try
List things on your wish list of desires that are just for you. E.g. hiking, art or craft project, swimming, yoga, volunteering, etc. and make plans to get some contact groups in your area

_____

_____

_____

_____

12. EMPOWERMENT (WHOLEHEARTED LIVING):

"Just when the caterpillar thought her life was over, she began to fly"
-author unknown

When I finally learnt to accept the things I could not change, and take control of the things I could change, my life after loss dramatically changed. This is why I remind you, the reader, throughout, that this is your grief journey to own. No one can tell you when, why, or how long. This is your story and the people in your past, who have been gifted to you to be a part of it, would want you to continue in loving memory to LIVE YOUR LIFE!

So what does that look like for you? How do you want to spend your days, even if it looks dramatically different from your current situation? I know for me there are many strong empowerment words that come up now, that for me (before loss) I would not have written down all those years ago.

I wanted different things, what I thought were important to me to do, have, achieve in my life are no longer even on the radar. So my final request for you is to take some quiet time to jot down some keywords that embrace your desires now, moving forward. For your life. Not for those around you, but for your soul. How do you want to be remembered? How do you wish to make people feel? What lessons have you learnt that may help your future generations deal with grief?

_____

_____

_____

I will leave you with a few EMPOWERMENT words of mine... soul strategies that pull me toward living my best, wholehearted life beyond grief and loss.

> **INTENTIONAL   MINDFUL**
>
> **AUTHENTIC**
>
> **PASSIONATE**
>
> **KIND**
>
> **HELPFUL   HONOURING**
>
> **LOYAL   ADVENTUROUS**
>
> –Xo Rachel

...In Closing

Everyone will experience grief
At some stage or another,
We need to be more aware
And be gentle to each other.

You might be at work
Or in a classroom
Or waiting in a line,
Beside someone who is grieving,
Who is wishing for more time.

The lesson and the gift
Is that we only have one chance.
So my teaching to you is
Don't wait to enjoy,
Life's magical dance.

This life is too precious,
Be grateful for your loved ones,
And always hold them tight,
Say I love and appreciate you,
Let your story be your light.

Rachel Pope

In Loving Memory
Of My Valiant Men

Brian John Roberts   *01/10/1944 ~ 28/03/1992*
Brett Stephen Roberts   *28/02/1966 ~ 05/02/2000*
Raymond Murray Pope   *11/09/1965 ~ 05/10/2012*

> *"Go Easy
> Step Lightly
> Stay Free"*
>
> —The Clash

www.ingramcontent.com/pod-product-compliance
Lightning Source LLC
Chambersburg PA
CBHW031420290426
44110CB00011B/459